Intelligent Guide

MW01198892

The Northern Rhône

January 2018 edition

Wines of The Northern Rhône

Benjamin Lewin MW
Copyright © 2018 Benjamin Lewin
Vendange Press
www.vendangepress.com

Preface

The first part of this guide discusses the Northern Rhône and its wines; the second part presents individual profiles of leading producers, and mini-profiles of many estates. The basic idea is that the first part explains the character and range of the wines, and the second part shows how each winemaker interprets that character. The *Guide to the Southern Rhône* applies the same approach to the region immediately to the south.

In the first part I address the nature of the wines made today and ask how this has changed, how it's driven by tradition or competition, and how styles may evolve in the future. I show how the wines are related to the terroir and to the types of grape varieties that are grown, and I explain the classification system. For each part of the region, I suggest reference wines that I believe typify the area; in some cases, where there is a split between, for example, modernists and traditionalists, there may be wines from each camp.

There's no single definition for what constitutes a top producer. Leading producers range from those who are so prominent as to represent the common public face of an appellation to those who demonstrate an unexpected potential on a tiny scale. The producers profiled in the guide should represent the best of both tradition and innovation in wine in the region

In the profiles, I have tried to give a sense of each producer's aims for his wines, of the personality and philosophy behind them—to meet the person who makes the wine, as it were, as much as to review the wines themselves. For each producer I suggest reference wines that are a good starting point for understanding his style. Most of the producers welcome visits, although some require appointments: details are in the profiles.

The guide is based on many visits to the region over recent years. I owe an enormous debt to the many producers who cooperated in this venture by engaging in discussion and opening innumerable bottles for tasting. This guide would not have been possible without them.

Benjamin Lewin

How to read the producer profiles

The second part of this guide consists of profiles of individual wine producers. Each profile shows a sample label, a picture of the winery, and details of production, followed by a description of the producer and winemaker. The producer's rating (from one to four stars) is shown to the right of the name.

The profiles are organized geographically, and each group of profiles is preceded by a map showing the locations of starred producers to help plan itineraries.

A full list of the symbols used in the profiles appears at the start of the profile section. This is an example of a profile:

Hospices de Beaune

VOLNAY
Premier Cru
Appellation Volnay Contrôlée
Cuvée Blondeau

Mis en bouteille par
Jean-Luc Aegerter
Négociant-Éleveur à 21700 Nuits-Saint-Georges

13 % vol.   Produit de France   750 ml

Hotel Dieu, Beaune, France
address

03 80 24 44 02

Catherine Guillemot

@ catherine.guillemot@ch-beaune.fr

Corton principal AOP

Beaune 1er, Nicolas Rolin
red reference wine

Corton Charlemagne, Charlotte Dumay
white reference wine

www.hospices-de-beaune.com

details of producer
60 ha; 400,000 bottles
vineyards & production

The Hospices de Beaune was founded in 1443 by Nicolas Rolin, chancellor of Burgundy, as a hospital for the poor. Standing in the heart of Beaune, the original buildings of the Hotel Dieu, now converted into a museum, surround a courtyard where an annual auction of wines was first held in 1859. The wines come from vineyards held as part of the endowment of the Hospices, and are sold in November to negociants who then take possession of the barrels and mature the wines in their own styles. (Today the auction is held in the modern covered marketplace opposite the Hotel Dieu.) There are 45 cuvées (32 red and 13 white); most come from premier or grand crus from the Côte de Beaune or Côte de Nuits, but because holdings are small (depending on past donations of land to the Hospices) many cuvées consist of blends from different crus (and are identified by brand names). The vines are cultivated, and the wine is made, by the Hospices. For some years the vineyards of the Hospices were not tended as carefully as they might have been, and the winemaking was less than perfect, but the appointment of a new régisseur has led to improvements in the present century. The name of the Hospices is only a starting point, because each negociant stamps his own style on the barriques he buys.

Contents

Overview of the Rhône

The river Rhône flows south from Lake Geneva across Savoie, before turning west to Lyon; then it flows more or less directly south for two hundred miles before debouching into the Mediterranean near Marseilles. Wine is produced all along the Rhône from below Lyon to the south of Avignon. Production divides naturally into two regions, the Northern Rhône and Southern Rhône, which are about as distant and distinct from one another as they are from Beaujolais to their north. There is a gap of about 30 miles between the regions.

The major difference between north and south is driven by climate: the Northern Rhône is only a little warmer than Burgundy, but the Southern Rhône belongs to the warm south. It's a measure of the difference that chaptalization (adding sugar before fermentation) is allowed in the Northern Rhône, but is forbidden in the south. The grape varieties in the north and south are different, but both are definitely red wine country: white wine production is only about 10%. The difference is eloquently put by Ralph Garcin at Maison Jaboulet: "For me the Rhône is ying and yang, it has two heads, Syrah and Grenache, the people are different, there is the north and there is the south."

Although the skinny band of the Northern Rhône extends for more than fifty miles, and the Southern Rhône encompasses a much wider area, spreading far beyond both banks of the river, each region is relatively homogeneous so far as vintage conditions go. It would be unusual to see vintage reports distinguishing one part of the Northern Rhône from another, or one part of the Southern Rhône from another,

The Rhône is an old winemaking region. Several panels were devoted to viticulture and vinification in a mosaic showing the agricultural calendar in the third century C.E., discovered in a Roman villa near Vienne. These included treading the grapes (left), operating a wine press (center), and producing amphorae for storage (right).

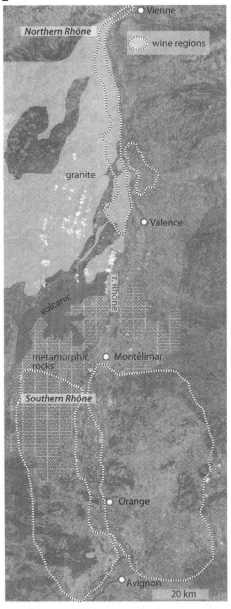

The river Rhône is the dividing line between metamorphic or volcanic rocks (to the west) and sedimentary rocks (to the east). Soils are sedimentary except as indicated. Vineyards of the Northern Rhône are north of Valence; vineyards of the Southern Rhône are south of Montélimar.

but conditions can be different between the north and south, with one region more successful than the other in any particular year.

The Northern Rhône is dwarfed by the South. In terms of the Rhône as a whole, the North accounts for about 5% of all production. However, production in the North almost all comes from eight appellations, described as Crus in local terminology, whereas most of the production in the South comes from the wide area of the Côtes du Rhône and its surrounding regional appellations. The equivalent quality to the north comes from the Crus of the south—Châteauneuf-du-Pape is the best known—which account for about 8% of production.

Grape Varieties

A single variety dominates red wine in the Northern Rhône: Syrah is the sole black grape. Many imaginative ideas about Syrah's origins (the best perhaps being that it came from Shiraz in Persia) were disposed of by the discovery that it resulted from a (spontaneous) cross between the varieties Dureza and Mondeuse. Dureza comes from the Ardèche (the area to the west of the Rhône), and Mondeuse comes from Savoie (towards the Alps to the east). This suggests that Syrah originated at the intersection, which is to say in the Northern Rhône.

But Syrah today may not be exactly the same as Syrah a century or so ago. Until the nineteenth century, the traditional black varieties were called Sérine in Côte Rôtie and Petite Sirrah in Hermitage; they were recognized as being the same variety only in 1846. These old cultivars now represent less than 10% of plantings: since the 1970s they have been replaced by modern clones—with mixed results, as the new clones generally have larger berries and are more productive.

There's some disagreement as to whether Sérine is merely local patois for Syrah in Côte Rôtie, or whether it represents a distinct subcultivar, but Pierre Gaillard is quite clear about it. "When I started in the 1980s, we had two different types of Syrah. One with round berries gave more alcohol and tannins; but Sérine had more ovoid berries. When they started to make the selection with clones, most of the Sérine had virus, so the clones mostly came from Hermitage (with the round berries). But now we have some clones from Sérine and people are planting them. Sérine gives a bit less structure but more complexity in the aromas and flavors."

For whites, Viognier is the only grape variety in Condrieu and Château-Grillet, the white wine appellations at the north of the region. It is vinified as a monovarietal wine. The principal white grape changes for the appellations farther south to Marsanne, which is often blended with Roussanne, a related variety, but monovarietals of either variety are also made.

Grape Varieties in Capsule

Syrah is relatively deeply colored with good tannins. It has a tendency to become peppery when not completely ripe. It is usually vinified as a monovarietal.

Viognier is an aromatic white, often quite perfumed, usually vinified as a monovarietal. Styles vary widely, from highly oaked to aging only in stainless steel.

Marsanne is the workhouse white grape, with a tendency to bitterness. It is often blended with a little Roussanne.

Roussanne is the finest white grape, but generally more successful in the southern Rhône than northern Rhône.

One unusual feature of red wine production in the Rhône has been the inclusion of white grapes in red wine. Plantings of black and white grapevines were historically intermingled, and the grapes were fermented together. The practice was more common in the Northern Rhône, where regulations still allow up to 15% or 20% white grapes to be included. In Côte-Rôtie, Viognier can be used; elsewhere, the permitted white varieties are Marsanne and Roussanne. The practice is not common today, but it is still followed by a few top growers, most notably Guigal for some Côte Rôties. "I am convinced that the Viognier brings an interesting aromatic complexity and some fatness, but it is belief only," Philippe Guigal explains.

The inclusion (or not) of Viognier in Côte Rôtie today often seems to be as much a matter of history as philosophy. When there are white grapes intermingled with red, producers are happy to include them, but when they replant, it's most often just with Syrah. There's little dissent from the view that a small amount of Viognier can add aromatic complexity, but no strong belief either that it's necessary.

The situation is a bit different outside of Côte Rôtie because the white grape varieties are different, and it's permitted to make white wine from them. "Côte Rôtie is different because Viognier is an aromatic grape. For Hermitage it is different, Marsanne and Roussanne were useful to soften the tannins," says Jean-Louis Chave. But he believes the practice depended more on market forces. "In Hermitage it's possible to include up to 15% white (in the red). But it doesn't make sense. It was more because demand was more for red so you could increase red production (by including the white grapes) but 15% is way too much." Better tannin management today means that it's not necessary to soften the tannins of the black grapes, and the white wines are selling well, so almost all the reds of Hermitage, Crozes-Hermitage, and St. Joseph are now 100% Syrah.

Appellations

The vineyards of the Northern Rhône run along the steep hillsides of the river valley. The need to work vineyards manually was largely responsible for their decline in the twentieth century. Costs were so much higher than elsewhere that production from the slopes was not competitive. "Except for Hermitage, the vineyards were mostly abandoned in the 1970s, and the few vines that were left were old but mostly not in good condition," recollects Pierre Gaillard. "The wines of this region have character—whether we like it or not—and it was only in the late 1980s that people became prepared to pay for it. Ironically it was the introduction of herbicides that made it possible to work the terraces," he says.

There's interest in moving to organic viticulture, but the big difficulty is working the soil. "There's no mechanization. This area was saved by herbicides. Now it's a challenge to get off the herbicides," says Alberic Mazoyer at Domaine Alain Voge. The soils are poor enough that allowing unrestricted cover crops creates too much competition for the

Vineyards rise up sharply close to the river. Courtesy Guigal.

6

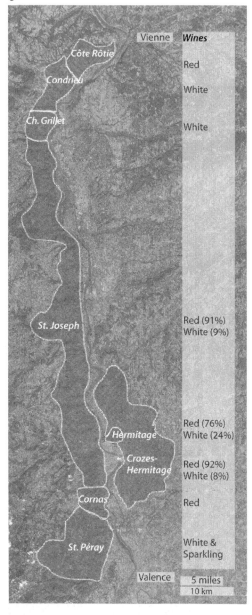

	Wines
Vienne	
Côte Rôtie	Red
Condrieu	White
Ch. Grillet	White
St. Joseph	Red (91%) White (9%)
Hermitage	Red (76%) White (24%)
Crozes-Hermitage	Red (92%) White (8%)
Cornas	Red
St. Péray	White & Sparkling
Valence	

5 miles
10 km

The northern Rhône is a skinny band of vineyards running along the river for fifty miles from Vienne to Valence.

vines. But weed control by manual means is backbreaking on the steep terraces—and expensive. "It takes 1000 hours to work a hectare here. We are in France—you can imagine the cost per hour!" says Alberic. In spite of this, almost half of the producers in this guide are organic.

Most of the wine-growing regions are classified as AOP; six of the eight appellations lie on the western side of the river, with only Hermitage and Crozes-Hermitage on the eastern side. Some outlying areas (often on adjoining flat land) are classified as IGP Collines Rhodaniennes. The best appellations for red wines are Côte Rôtie, near Vienne, and Hermitage, at a turn in the river a bit north of Valence. These are the most prestigious appellations in the entire Rhône, and together amount to about 10% of production. The reds of Crozes-Hermitage, St. Joseph, and Cornas are not as fine: Crozes-Hermitage and St. Joseph are the big producers, accounting for 80% of northern Rhône wines.

Syrah is grown in all appellations except Condrieu, Château-Grillet, and St. Péray, which make only white wine. The change in white varieties going south means there's a stylistic difference between Condrieu or Château Grillet and the white wines of the other appellations. Cornas produces only red wine.

Côte Rôtie

One word describes the terroir of the best sites in the Northern Rhône: granite. Depending on the minerals that were present when granite was formed as the rocks cooled, it can have many different colors, as seen in Côte Rôtie. Although Côte Rôtie means "roasted slope," the appellation is really more a series of slopes, rising up from the river. The best vineyards are on the slopes opposite the town of Ampuis, where the two most celebrated lieu-dits of the Côte Rôtie take their

Côte Rôtie extends for 3 km along the west bank of the Rhône. The lieu-dits of Côte Brune and Côte Blonde are just above the town of Ampuis, and mark the division between the terroirs of the southern and northern halves.

The heart of Côte Rôtie is above the town of Ampuis. Slopes rise up steeply from the Rhône.

names from the colors of the minerals. Just above Ampuis, the rocks are a mixture of muscovite (white mica) and biotite (black mica), which together give the brown impression that led to the name Côte Brune. Just south of the town, there is white-colored gneiss, which gave rise to the name Côte Blonde. Going on south, the terroir is pure granite. But this should not be taken to mean impenetrable: in fact, the granite is quite friable, and if you hit one of the rocks lying on the surface, it usually breaks up into smaller pieces quite easily.

Although today Côte Rôtie has a reputation to match Hermitage, the other great name in the Northern Rhône, it was much less well known until recently. During the nineteenth century, Côte Rôtie used to sell at around half the price of Hermitage, but after the second world war, it was being sold off for pennies. Vineyard plantings have gone up and down, from 420 ha in 1907, to 72 ha in 1973, and back up to 242 ha today. Much of the revival is due to the halo effect of Marcel Guigal's series of splendid single vineyard bottlings starting in the 1970s. Until then, most wine was handled by negociants or sold off in bulk; little Côte Rôtie was bottled by growers.

There is more variation in terroir here than in the more compact hill of Hermitage. The plateau at the top of Côte Rôtie is the least distinguished terroir. The ravine of Reynaud is the dividing line between Côte Brune and Côte Blonde. Strictly speaking, Côte Brune and Côte Blonde originated as merely two of the 73 lieu-dits on the Côte Rôtie,

The steep slope of Côte Rôtie requires terraces every few rows, and vines are grown as individual bushes. Courtesy Inter-Rhône, Christophe Grilhé.

but the terms have become widely used to distinguish the northern and southern parts of the appellation. The general difference in terroirs between north and south is that Côte Brune has harder rocks, with more schist, and iron-rich soils, giving the typically taut, structured quality of volcanic terrain. Côte Blonde has more friable granite, and the wine tends to be fine and elegant, with less evident tannic structure. This soil extends into Condrieu.

Côte Rôtie offers the most rounded expression of Syrah in the Rhône. Usually it is softer than Hermitage, although generalizing is difficult given the difference between Côte Brune and Côte Blonde, and variations in winemaking, extending from destemming to including Viognier. The tradition in the Rhône has been to blend from different terroirs in order to increase complexity. Sometimes, of course, it's a matter of necessity: a producer may have many small lots in different locations. As Pierre Gaillard comments, "You have to do vinification terroir by terroir because of differing maturities. The tradition in Côte Rôtie is to make a blend of Côte Brune and Côte Blonde. There are economic arguments to make small and rare lots, but if you are going to stay in the appellation system, it is best to follow the traditions of the vineyards."

The game changer was Guigal's introduction of single vineyard wines that attracted wide critical acclaim. In addition to focusing on terroir, Guigal introduced a new style, with long maturation in new

Individual vines are densely planted. Each has a supporting pyramid.

oak. La Mouline, La Turque, and La Landonne are splendid wines that stand on their own merits, but it is fair to say that their character is definitely powerful compared to the more delicate, sometimes almost perfumed, wines that traditionalists regard as typical of Côte Rôtie. However, critics might remember that Côte Rôtie was in desperate straits before Guigal spurred its revival.

There's no clear consensus on the use of new oak, although Guigal definitely started a trend. "I don't think old versus new oak is a debate now, although it used to be. I am the first to say new oak can be good or bad for wine," Philippe Guigal says. "We have a single variety—Syrah—and it can be very powerful. By using new oak we have oxidation, which affects the structure of the wines. I cannot change the quantity of tannins, but by doing long aging, for 36-42 months for the Côte Rôties, I can change the quality of the tannins. The wines will show as more subtle and soft when young—and they will age for more than ten years. Using new oak barrels, it's not the aromas that are essential, it's the work on the tannins, making the wine ready to drink."

Reference Wines for Côte Rôtie

Maison Guigal, Château d'Ampuis
René Rostaing, Côte Blonde
Clusel-Roch, Les Grandes Places
Maison Guigal, Château d'Ampuis
Domaine Jasmin

The impetus from Guigal's success means that the tradition of making a single wine by blending different parts of Côte Rôtie has now given way to a focus on expressing differences. Most producers now have multiple cuvées. Sometimes the distinction is terroir, sometimes it is vine age, sometimes it is just selection. Styles vary from perfumed, lacy, and elegant, to powerful and spicy, but the common feature should be a certain smoothness. There's almost always a definite step up in quality when Côte Rôtie comes from a lieu-dit; of course, the effect may really be more the other way round, that is, the interest of the regular bottling has been reduced by removing the best lots. I wonder if that is why recently I have had more Côte Rôties that have disappointed me by lacking that traditional plushness.

Seyssuel

Before moving on south from Côte Rôtie, we need to make a detour farther up the Rhône, to Seyssuel, north of Vienne. Known as Saxeolum during the Roman era, Seyssuel may have been the source of the wines of Vienne that enjoyed a high reputation during the Middle Ages. Destroyed by phylloxera at the end of the nineteenth century, the Seyssuel vineyards fell into disarray, and were revived only at the instigation of Pierre Gaillard, who in 1996 persuaded Yves Cuilleron and François Villard to join him in recreating the old vineyards. Under the name of Vins de Vienne, they replanted vineyards and started to produce wines, naming the cuvées for the wines from the area that were famous in the Roman era.

The vineyards are on the east bank of the Rhône, at a point where the river is at its narrowest. The terroir is similar to the Côte Brune, based on schist; when they planted Seyssuel, they had to use a bulldozer and ripper to break up the ground. However, whereas Côte Rôtie

The old château of the archbishop at Seyssuel is now surrounded by the restored vineyards, planted with the same pyramidal pruning as Côte Rôtie.

faces southeast, on the opposite side of the river Seyssuel faces more southwest. It's better protected from the wind, which is stronger at Côte Rôtie. In addition to Vins de Vienne, each of the three founders has taken one hectare of vines to make their own wine. Now other vignerons have also established vineyards in the area, and Seyssuel counts more than a dozen producers today, with 30-40 ha of vineyards. (Supposedly the few vignerons still working at Seyssuel were asked if they wanted to be included in Côte Rôtie when the appellation was created, but they declined. So Seyssuel falls under the IGP of Collines Rhodaniennes.)

I have been impressed with the wines of Seyssuel. The reds are pure Syrah (there are also some whites from Viognier). They show a refined quality, at least as fine as Côte Rôtie; perhaps, if you are looking for a distinction, a little less round and more precise. They have an unobtrusive structure and a tendency towards silkiness. In each pairwise comparison of wines from the same producer, the wine from Seyssuel seems at least as complex aromatically as the Côte Rôtie, and I sometimes find the texture to be finer. The Sotanum cuvée from Vins de Vienne is, of course, the reference point.

Condrieu & Château Grillet

Returning to the main drag of the Northern Rhône, Côte Blonde runs into Condrieu, which makes only white wine. Wine has been produced at Condrieu since the Roman era, and in the Middle Ages it was shipped down the river to the popes in Avignon. However, by the end of the 1960s, Condrieu, together with its tiny neighbor, Château-Grillet, had what amounted to the last few hectares of Viognier in the world. A revival started in the 1980s, and today Condrieu has 140 ha planted out of a potential area of 262 ha. The AOP turned back towards quality when its size was reduced by about a third in 1986 by excluding all terrain above 300m elevation. Now there are also significant plantings of Viognier elsewhere in the Rhône and in Languedoc.

A strongly aromatic variety, Viognier can be perfumed and floral, even musky. With relatively low acidity and high alcohol, it is best drunk young. There are enormous quality differences between a top Condrieu with intense aromas and palate, and lesser versions, where the perfume may outrun the fruits; in short Viognier is a variety that needs concentrated fruits to give good balance against its perfumed background. Viognier made from inferior clones that give high yields of less aromatic fruit (of which a good number were planted when its popularity revived) can be clumsy. It can be vinified in a variety of styles from fresh and clean to heavily oaked; this makes it difficult to get a bead on any consistent style for Condrieu.

The main stylistic factors in winemaking are whether to perform malolactic fermentation and whether and what type of oak to use. Modernists believe in oak, but traditionalists are against it. Modernist Yves Cuilleron argues that, "In the nineteenth century Condrieu was vinified in new oak. Today we use a bit less than 20% except for the vins de garde." He believes that Condrieu's potential for aging is underestimated. "Condrieu has a reputation for (lack of) aging that I think is wrong. Amateurs like the aroma of the young wine, but for me it's a wine with minerality that can age, although of course it changes, and the aromatic complexity becomes different."

Known for the elegance of his wines, René Rostaing has strong views on the subject. "Oak destroys the typicity of Viognier. In France we make wine with grapes, not oak. I'm the adversary of new oak. The source of oak is not important—it's only an instrument. When I am President of the French Republic, new oak will be forbidden in Condrieu." My own view is that Viognier loses its character if too much

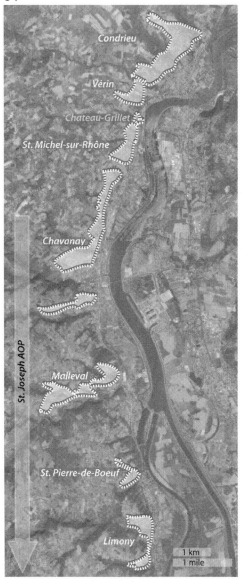

The Condrieu AOP includes 7 villages extending from Condrieu itself to Limony. The three northern villages (Condrieu, Vérin, and St. Michel-sur-Rhône) were included in the original appellation in 1940. The four southern villages were added later and also form the northern part of the St. Joseph AOP.

new oak is used, and for me, too much means any detectable sensation of new oak, because it clashes with the natural aromatics of the grape.

Château-Grillet is an enclave surrounded by Condrieu. Even given its high reputation, it's unclear why this single vineyard should have been picked out as a separate AOP (rather than perhaps being marked as a "Cru" of Condrieu). This tiny appellation of 3.5 ha was the property of the Neyret-Gachet family until it was sold to François Pinault (of Château Latour) in 2011. The wine has always been rare and expensive, and although like Condrieu it is made exclusively from Viognier, it has been considered quite distinct: wine that should not be drunk young, but should have at least a decade's age. Because Château-Grillet is a monopole, it's impossible to say whether its character, which shows more minerality than Condrieu, is intrinsic to the terroir or depends on specific features of viticulture and vinification.

Maps usually show a linear progression of appellations down the Rhône: Côte Rôtie - Condrieu - Château-Grillet - St. Joseph, which is how the appellations started, but today there is some overlap because the appellations have been extended. Condrieu was originally three villages at the northern end, but has been extended farther south by four villages. And today St. Joseph is so extended that its northern part overlaps with the southern part of Condrieu: from Chavanay to Limony, growers may plant Viognier to make Condrieu, Syrah to make St. Joseph red, or Marsanne and Roussanne to make St. Joseph white. "In the same village you may have Marsanne to make St. Joseph and Viognier to make Condrieu. The grapes decide the appellation. It's totally crazy," says Jean-Louis Chave, whose family has been making wine in St. Joseph for centuries.

The wines from the northern part of the Condrieu appellation are richer, bringing out the floral, sometimes exotic, quality of Viognier, with pears, apricots, and honey. In the southern villages, the style is tighter and more mineral. There is also a range from fully dry to sweet wines, going all the way to late harvest, so in short, there is no easy generalization about style. If you really want to see the typicity of Viognier, however, stick to dry wines or to the just off-dry. Aging is a mixed bag: those early, floral, aromatics disappear, and you have to wait for something else to replace them. Its aromatics make Viognier a wine that to my mind can be difficult to match with food: it's a splendid aperitif, although on the richer side. It's sometimes claimed to be good with foods that are difficult to match with other white wines, such as asparagus and artichoke.

Hermitage

Hermitage has always been the great name in the Rhône, although its role has changed. Ever since the eighteenth century, Hermitage was regularly sold to negociants in Bordeaux or Burgundy to strengthen their wines. During the nineteenth century, as much as 80% of the production of Hermitage was bought by the Bordeaux wine trade. This had to stop after new regulations came into effect at the start of the twentieth century, but the wine continued to be sold in bulk. The white wine had a higher reputation than the red; in fact, negociants were compelled to buy the red in order to obtain the white. Things more or less collapsed after the first world war, with a large part of production moving from small growers to a cooperative, and only four negociants handling the wines. Most of the wine was sold to negociants until the revival of the 1970s. By then, the appellation was almost fully planted. Today about three quarters of production is red.

Because Hermitage is a single hill, its geography restricts the size of the appellation to about 135 ha. It consists of a granitic outcrop, an anomaly that is virtually the only granite on the east side of the river, created when the river changed its course long ago to flow round the west instead of the east side of the hill. The hill rises directly up steeply above the town of Tain l'Hermitage (originally called Tain until it was renamed to reflect the glory of the wine), with houses extending right up to its base. Retaining walls are used to hold in the topsoil. Southern exposure is an important feature, protecting the vineyards from the north wind and giving good sunlight. "Like the Pinot Noir in Burgundy, we're at the northern extreme of the Syrah's ripening here at Hermitage," according to Jean-Louis Chave, one of the top producers.

There is some variation in terroir around the hill. Granite at the western end changes to stones resulting from glacial deposits at the eastern side. Running round the hill are a series of *climats*, each with its own characteristics. The top climats are the granite-driven sites at the west: Les Bessards, Le Méal, and l'Hermite. If Hermitage was part of Burgundy, many or all of the lieu-dits would be bottled as separate wines, but the tradition here has been more towards blending. Jean-Louis Chave, who is widely acknowledged as the master of blending, explains why Hermitage is different from Burgundy: "What was local in 1936 when the AOP was created? For sure, what was local in Burgundy was to have Crus. In 1936 they thought about having Crus here, but what was local here was to blend wine from different sites to make

Looking north along the Rhône, the hill of Hermitage stands out for its southern exposure. Rising up immediately behind the town of Tain l'Hermitage, vineyards extend to 300m altitude. The northern part of Crozes-Hermitage is also hilly. St. Joseph is on the west side of the river.

the Hermitage. It's not like in Burgundy where there are small differences reflected between the Crus, here there is a very big difference from granite to loess—so at the end the question is: what is Hermitage? For sure, you can make wine from Les Bessards or other plots, but they are not Hermitage, they are Bessards etc."

This remains a lively argument in Hermitage. Philippe Guigal sees a difference with Côte Rôtie. "On the heritage, I think it is important to make people realize that, like Burgundy, we have one of the most important precision of terroirs in Côte Rôtie. Many people have followed the example of vineyard bottlings. But also look at Hermitage. Chapoutier says the real Hermitage is a bottling of individual terroirs, but Chave believes that it is a blend. In Côte Rôtie, I like the idea of single vineyards very much. Although there is a difference between south and north, in a blind tasting you end up by saying, this is Côte Rôtie. But for me Hermitage is a melting pot." Following this line of thought, Guigal's top Hermitage is a blend from very old vines, coming from the Grippat vineyards that they purchased a few years ago. The Ex Voto red Hermitage comes from 60-year-old vines from four climats; the white comes from the oldest vines of Les Murets, planted around 1910-1920, together with some from L'Hermite. White Hermitage can be long lived. Philippe says of the white Ex Voto that, "I believe like Chave that we will probably drink our reds before our whites; this should last for twenty years."

If there is any single definition of the character of Hermitage, it is probably Chave's cuvée, with its backbone coming from Les Bessards. "Every year we ask the same question: 'What should Hermitage be like given the conditions of that particular year?'" says Jean-Louis. Assessing the effect of terroir is difficult in Hermitage, because relatively few producers make separate cuvées. But a barrel tasting at Chave is an education in terroirs. The striking differences immediately make Jean-Louis's point about the extent of terroir differences compared to Burgundy. "You have to balance the character of the vintage: in a soft year you need more backbone; in a year that gives tight wine, the flesh is more important. In a cool year Le Méal will be more important in the

The Climats of Hermitage

The most tannic wine for most producers usually comes from *Les Bessards*, which is the backbone of several important Hermitage bottlings. At Chave, it's the most concentrated, tannic, and tight: for me, this is the barrel sample that most directly fits my image of Hermitage.

Just to the east of Les Bessards, turning from southwest to pure south-facing, lies *Le Méal*, where small stones near the surface mean it is always hotter than Les Bessards. Less granite brings a less austere, fuller, fruitier, impression. Chave's sample gives a great impression of refinement.

L'Hermite is above Les Bessards and Le Méal; soils vary more here, and it is planted with a mix of white as well as red grapes. Chave's barrel is less concentrated than Les Bessards, but smoother and more refined.

At the very top of the hill, *Les Grandes Vignes* does not ripen as reliably as l'Hermite, Le Méal, and Les Bessards below it.

Farther round the hill, at the northern limit, *Rocoule* is quite structured, but aromatic; *Péléat* just below is softer and rounder; and *Beaume* farther west is more animal.

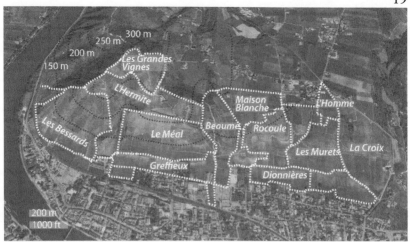

Hermitage is divided into about twenty lieu-dits. The most important are named here.

blend than Les Bessards, in a warm year it will be the other way round. What is important is the balance at the end," Jean-Louis says.

Another important blended wine, which for many years defined Hermitage, is Jaboulet's La Chapelle. The name comes from the chapel that stands on Jaboulet's part of Les Bessards (reputedly constructed by the Chevalier de Sterimberg, the original hermit in the thirteenth century). "What made Hermitage famous fifty years ago was La Chapelle, but it's a commercial name, not a vineyard, and it was 1,500 bottles; in a small place like Hermitage, this was a big quantity, and it was only possible because of blending," Jean-Louis explains. The blend was heavily based on the large holding of Le Méal that Louis Jaboulet built up over three decades starting in the 1950s. La Chapelle was one of the great wines of Hermitage through the 1960s, and the 1961 is legendary, but its concentration declined through the nineties when quantity increased. Quality began to recover after Jaboulet was sold in 2006 to the Frey family (who own Château La Lagune in the Médoc).

Ownership of Hermitage is quite concentrated, with two thirds held by the large firms of Chapoutier, Jaboulet, and Delas, or bottled by the cooperative (the Cave de Tain, which owns 21 ha). The largest holder is Chapoutier, which controls almost a quarter of the Hermitage hill, owning 26 ha, as well as leasing a further 5 ha. The major production is under a brand name, Monier de la Sizeranne, but Chapoutier also produce one of the few examples of a vineyard series, comprising Les Greffieux, Le Méal, L'Hermite, and Le Pavillon. Here is a direct reflection of the reputation of each plot in the ascending price of the series (Le Pavillon comes from Les Bessards). The step up in quality from Monier de la Sizeranne to the vineyard plots is striking. On the one hand, it makes you wish there were more examples where expression of terroir could be represented; on the other, it makes the point that even on the fabled hill, some plots of Hermitage are less equal than others. However, relatively few of the more than twenty producers of Hermitage produce individual vineyard wines.

Red Hermitage can be stern when young, but very long-lived, developing savory flavors resembling Bordeaux after ten or twenty years. That was a fair assessment until the recent warming trend. Since then there has been something of a move here as everywhere else to wines that are more attractive when young, displaying forward, primary fruits. With regards to producing wines that are easier to drink, I realize it's damned if you do, and damned if you don't, but I do wonder whether Hermitage should ever be easy and approachable? Syrah as a grape certainly has the potential to produce extremely lush wines; Australian Shiraz (the New World name for Syrah) can be quite overwhelming in its powerful aromatics of black fruits. But "we can't make Shiraz and they (Australians) can't make Northern Rhône Syrah, it's just impossible. They are completely different wines made from the same grape," says Ralph Garcin. The classic description of red Hermitage was always "pepper," associated with something short of what would today be regarded as real ripeness. This is rare now, as the expression of Syrah in Hermitage has moved more in the direction of black plums. Yet most wines still retain good freshness.

Reference Wines for Hermitage
Red
Jean-Louis Chave
Jaboulet, La Chapelle
Domaine Belle
Maison Delas Frères, Domaine des Tourrettes
White
Jean-Louis Chave
Jaboulet, Chevalier Sterimberg
Marc Sorrel, Les Rocoules
Michel Ferraton Les Miaux

Crozes Hermitage

Southern exposure, hillside slopes, and granitic soil explain Hermitage's unique quality. Crozes-Hermitage is much larger, spread out in a semicircle, with the hill of Hermitage at the bull's eye. Only a small proportion of Crozes-Hermitage is produced by domains actually in the appellation. More than half comes from small growers who send their grapes to the cooperative at Tain l'Hermitage, another cooperative accounts for a further 10%, and many of the remaining vineyards are owned by the large negociants (Chapoutier, Jaboulet, and Delas). Probably less than 20% actually comes from producers whose focus is on Crozes-Hermitage.

Like many other appellations in the Northern Rhône, Crozes-Hermitage started as a small area immediately around the village, just north of Hermitage. As it became successful, it expanded into the surrounding areas. Crozes-Hermitage is now the largest appellation in the Northern Rhône, but it's fair to say that quality is more or less proportional to distance from the original village. There's a split personality between the northern and southern parts of the appellation. The steep hillside vineyards based on granite hills to the north give taut wines, whereas the southern plain of Chassis gives wines that are simpler and fruitier. None of this, however, is of much relevance to the consumer, since so far as the label is concerned, Crozes-Hermitage is Crozes-Hermitage. The producer's name is the more important guide.

It's hard to find growers who emphasize expression of local terroir. Philippe Belle is an exception—he even has examples of the soils from different terroirs in his tasting room—and his cuvées highlight the characteristics of each terroir. Coming from pebbly terroir on the plain of Chassis, Les Pierelles has the most forward fruits—"Everything is destemmed, because we want fruit," says Philippe—but the structural underpinning brings some character and shows that the plain doesn't have to be as simple as it often is. The grapes for Cuvée Louis Belle (from white clay terroir around the winery in Larnage) and Roche Pierre (granitic terroir) are partially destemmed, "Because these are vins de terroir." Moving into more granitic terroir there is an increasingly taut edge to the fruits. Crozes-Hermitage is never going to compete with Hermitage—for one thing, most of the best growers produce both wines so Crozes will always be second—but the "granite" villages in the north deserve more overt recognition.

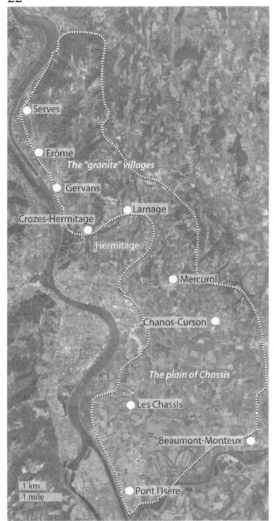

The northern part of Cro-
zes-Hermitage produces
more structured wines
from the four granite villages along the river; the
southern part produces
more fruit-forward wines
from the plain of Chassis.

The focus in Hermitage and Crozes-Hermitage is on Syrah, which is planted on the best granite terroirs; the white grapes of Marsanne and Roussanne are planted elsewhere *faute de mieux.* Roussanne is the finer grape, but is difficult to grow. Marsanne is the more widely grown; it does not do especially well on granite soils, but does better on the other soil types, such as clay and chalk. Often blended together, Marsanne and Roussanne make a dry wine with savory and herbal aromas and a nutty (sometimes bitter) taste. The overall impression is aromatic and a little perfumed, with a dry finish that emphasizes the

Reference Wines for Crozes Hermitage

Red

J.L. Chave Selection
Domaine Belle, Cuvée Louis Belle
Paul Jaboulet, Domaine de Roure
Maison Delas Frères, Le Clos
Domaine des Remizières, Cuvée Autrement

White

Paul Jaboulet, Domaine de Roure
Domaine Belle, Roche Blanche
Les Vins de Vienne, Amphore d'Argent

perfume. Marsanne (and Marsanne-Roussanne blends) tend to be dumb at first, often needing three or so years for flavor to emerge. One objective of winemaking is to control the (potential) bitter taste.

The chief exponent of Marsanne is Chapoutier, who makes a 100% varietal Hermitage. "The structure is the bitterness," says Michel Chapoutier, "Marsanne is the only grape variety that can live a long time without much acidity." "The bitterness is a mark of Marsanne: I call our whites, tannic white wines," says Alberic Mazoyer at Domaine Alain Voge. Guigal also makes a pure varietal, while Chave includes 15% or so Roussanne. The most important blended white wine in Hermitage is Jaboulet's Chevalier de Sterimberg, with about a third Roussanne. White Hermitage is usually reckoned to be at its best after about ten years. The problem with whites from Crozes-Hermitage is that there is often not enough fruit concentration to compensate for the low acidity.

Saint Joseph

Overlapping with Condrieu, St. Joseph extends 40 miles down the Rhône, where its southern end surrounds the town of Tour-non-sur-Rhône and faces Hermitage and Crozes-Hermitage. Originally this *was* the appellation in 1971, consisting of 97 ha in the villages immediately to the north and south of Tournon (from St.-Jean-de-Muzols to Mauves). Then it was expanded dramatically. "In the early 1990s, I saw the appellation of St. Joseph slipping away from its original values, due to quick over-expansion," says Jean-Louis Chave, who lately has been

The expansion of St. Joseph created an AOP with the most variability in the Northern Rhône. Vineyards run for 40 miles along the Rhône, extending inland from near the river to slopes with varying exposure. Courtesy Inter-Rhône, Christophe Grilhé.

replanting the vineyards that his family first cultivated in 1481. That is quite a mild statement considering the extent of the expansion into land that used to be only Côtes du Rhône. St. Joseph grew to 540 ha in 1989; today it is 1,200 ha. This is the old phenomenon of *fureur de planting*, historically leading to a boom and bust cycle. The local Syndicat has finally taken the situation in hand and proposes to remove unsuitable vineyards from the appellation—but only starting in 2021!

With the appellation extending for 40 miles along the river, it is not surprising that there is a difference between the northern and southern parts. "In St. Joseph there are years that are better in the south versus the north, but the soils are relatively homogeneous," says Yves Cuilleron. The differences are in exposure and elevation, and a warmer climate in the south. Quality has been erratic, with one significant factor being that many vineyards are so recently planted. "The main difficulty in St. Joseph is that we have two poles," says Philippe Guigal, "Although Guigal is in the north, our St. Joseph is all from the south." The original St. Joseph consisted of five valleys where the rivers created hills facing south or southeast. In the expanded appellation, the vineyards tend to face east: "It's not very logical, exposure should have been a criterion in defining the appellation," says Claire Darnaud McKerrow at Delas Frères.

References Wines for St. Joseph

Red

Domaine André Perret, Les Grisières
Domaine Belle, Les Rivoires
Maison Guigal, Vigne de l'Hospice
Yves Cuilleron, Les Sérines
Delas Frères, Saint Epine
J. J. Chave Selection, Offerus

White

Yves Cuilleron, Saint Pierre
Michel Ferraton Père & Fils, La Source

The best wines come from established vineyards in the heart of the old appellation, known locally as the "berceau" [cradle] of St. Joseph. Some are in fact better than the average Hermitage (and priced accordingly), such as Chapoutier's Les Granits (both red and white), Delas's L'Epine, and Guigal's Vigne de l'Hospice. The last is especially interesting, coming from a hillside directly across the river from Hermitage. This is the other part of what was originally one massive granite outcrop, before the river cut through, leaving 20% on the west bank, with the other 80% forming the hill of Hermitage on the east bank. If the river had not switched from one side of the hill to the other, l'Hospice would be part of the same block as Hermitage.

It's an interesting question whether to choose St. Joseph or Crozes Hermitage when faced with a choice from unknown producers. The general advice from producers is that St. Joseph is a less risky bet. "Between St. Joseph and Crozes Hermitage, St. Joseph is safer, it is more traditional. The difference is due to the fact that most of Crozes Hermitage is on the plain of Chassis, whereas most of St. Joseph is a slope," says Jacques Grange of Delas Frères.

Cornas

The next village down the river, Cornas often has more character, but exactly what is that character? With only just over a hundred hectares of vineyards, and production exclusively of reds, Cornas has a much sharper focus than St. Joseph. A small area almost at the south of the Northern Rhône, it is protected by hills just to the north that make

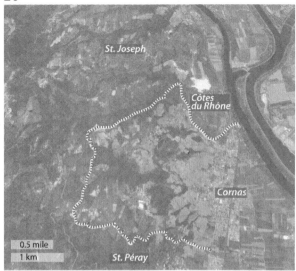

Cornas is an appellation of 125 ha centered on the village.

the main climatic factor the warm wind from the south; Cornas usually ripens a week earlier than Hermitage. Green oaks and junipers mark the point of transition in Cornas to Mediterranean vegetation. Cornas is an exception to the usual rule that vintages are homogeneous in the Northern Rhône; it can do better than other appellations in poor years.

The modern era dates from 1956 when some important producers decided to bottle their own wines. Marcel Juge, Noël Verset, Auguste Clape, and others, made really characterful wines. Certainly there have been ups and downs in viticulture; there was a decline in the planted area, which fell to just over 50 ha in 1970, before rising steadily. The terraced vineyards start at the village (just above the Rhône at 110m elevation), rising up on hills that go up to about 420m. Like Burgundy, the feeling is that the best sites are in the middle of the slope, although there are some exceptions. "There's a big difference with altitude: more wind at the top, more water and humidity at the bottom, and an average 2°C temperature drop from bottom to top. Harvest can be three weeks later at the top than the bottom," says Cyril Courvoisier, viticulturalist at Jean-Luc Colombo before he started his own domain.

The warmer trend of recent years allows viticulture higher up the slope. "With climate change now it's possible to cultivate vineyards there. When Colombo planted land higher up in Cornas people said he was crazy, that the grapes would not ripen," Cyril recollects. But now the trend has been taken to extremes. There is concern that recent ex-

The village of Cornas is below the vineyards on the hills.

pansion right on to the top of the hills may adversely affect the typicity of Cornas. A good breeze in center slope can be a gale at the exposed summit. Standing in a vineyard at one point on the summit where the wind was absolutely howling, it was hard to believe that it would be possible for the vines to get through flowering, let along develop ripe berries. "When the appellation was defined, we did not expect people to go up there and plant," says Olivier Clape of Domaine Auguste Clape. The big question is really whether the reputation of Cornas can withstand the expansion into unsuitable terroirs.

Rustic is no longer a fair description of Cornas, but the wines remain sturdier than those of Hermitage or Côte Rôtie; certainly they tend to be well structured (which is why Cornas is often tasted last in comparisons). I often get high-toned aromatics in Cornas, sometimes showing as truffles, but I haven't so far identified any common origin for this feature. "We don't want to impress with the concentration. We are in Cornas, it's difficult to make rosé (meaning that the fruits inevitably have a certain weight and toughness). We want purity of fruits and freshness," says Alberic Mazoyer at Domaine Alain Voge. Even at traditionalist Auguste Clape, whose wines for me define the tradition of the appellation, there is now a more approachable young vines bottling (aptly called Renaissance). There is absolutely no sign of new oak in the Clape cellars, and the traditional cuvée certainly needs time; about ten years would be right. At the other extreme, Jean-Luc Colombo was regarded as a young Turk when he introduced new oak into Cornas, about twenty years ago. "When my parents were criticized for making more sophisticated wine, people would say, this wine is not typical," Laure Colombo comments, but I would say that Colombo has won the argument: the modern style is now found throughout the appellation.

Modernists and Traditionalists in Cornas	
Traditionalists: little or no destemming, long cuvaison, little new wood	Frank Balthazar Auguste Clape Marcel Juge Corinne Lionet Robert Michel Noël Verset
Modernists: destemming, higher fermentation temperatures, punch-down, some new wood	Jean-Luc Colombo Domaine Courbis Alain Voge

Immediately to the south of Cornas, St. Péray (the southernmost appellation in the Northern Rhône), is a bit of an oddity: production is exclusively white, from Marsanne and Roussanne, but this includes a proportion of sparkling wine. Production of sparkling wine started in the early nineteenth century, and the wine was quite well known at that time, but today it's mostly consumed locally, and little is exported. Certainly Marsanne and Roussanne are not obvious varieties from which to make sparkling wine, and today its production is dwindling (probably down to less than 15% of total). Indeed, total production in St. Péray is very small, and even the dry white wine remains the least well known of the Northern Rhône. In fact, St. Péray was in danger of extinction a few years back, when the local growers went to Jaboulet and Chapoutier and asked for help; by buying grapes and producing an appellation wine, the negociants rescued the appellation. The problem with St. Péray, however, is a certain lack of character compared with its northern neighbors: the wines can be pleasant in a soft, direct way, but they rarely take on much character.

Syrah & Granite

A single black variety, Syrah, is grown all along the Northern Rhône, yet the character of each appellation (or at least of the traditional heart of each appellation) is quite different. Even allowing for the fact that Côte Rôtie can include Viognier, that Hermitage, Crozes Hermitage, or St. Joseph can include Marsanne and Roussanne, and that Cornas is exclusively Syrah, this is a clear enough demonstration of the effect of terroir. Until the modern era, there may have been local differences in the cultivars of Syrah, but today the widespread introduction of clones means that growers all over the Northern Rhône are likely to be using

Outcrops of granite show the underlying terroir.

the same plant material (except for those who are skeptical about the character of the clones and prefer to perpetuate the heritage of their vineyards by selection massale). Jean-Louis Chave has a typically strong view on this. "The main clones of Syrah were selected in the eighties, and the aim at that time was to have more ripeness. We have at least 1%, sometimes 1.5%, less alcohol with our plants coming from selection massale than with clones. And with the very old vines we don't get to this crazy level of sugar. The old vines are less perfect than the clones, which all look the same, ripen the same way—and give the same wine at the end."

Most of the appellations of the Northern Rhône have now expanded well beyond their initial focus. The only exceptions are Hermitage (limited by the hill) and St. Péray (limited by lack of interest). It's taking the concept of the appellation to breaking point when it includes totally different areas, such as the granitic northern half of Crozes Hermitage and the alluvial southern plain. "We should have two appellations, Crozes and Crozes Hermitage," one producer told me (he asked not to be quoted by name!). If there were two such appellations, they would almost certainly have rather different reputations. Similarly the "berceau" of St. Joseph is of distinctly more interest than the new parts of the appellation. "It would be right for St. Joseph to accept that there are different levels, and to have Crus," says Jean-Louis Chave. Confusion about typicity probably prevents the best parts of the appellation from casting a halo over the weaker parts; indeed, the relationship may be the other way round, with the weaker parts of the appellation preventing recognition of the better villages.

While global warming has been pushing up alcohol levels everywhere, in some cases threatening to overwhelm the traditional style, it seems to have had less effect in the Northern Rhône. Most wines stay in a range between 13% and 13.5%, and retain their traditional freshness. The difference from the past is that all the alcohol is natural. "In the north thirty years ago we used to chaptalize every year, now not at all," says Laure Colombo. Philippe Guigal thinks global warming has been a benefit so far. "Lots of people talk about global warming. I'm very concerned about Châteauneuf-du-Pape with 16% alcohol. I prefer to have more Mourvèdre and to keep alcohol lower. In the Northern Rhône I have a strange answer: I prefer the situation today. Thirty years ago, we were harvesting in late September and chaptalizing every year. In the past we always harvested during or past the equinox when it often rains. Now with global warming we often harvest just before the strong rains of the equinox."

"The advantage of granite is that even in warm years the grapes do not become cooked," says Jean-Louis Chave. Excluding the unprecedented heat of 2003, the most testing vintage recently was 2009, which has produced unusually ripe wines, more popular with the public than 2010, which was more typical. "2009 is more of a consumer vintage; 2010 is more of a winemaker vintage that really reflects the appellations," says Olivier Clape. If 2009 were the limit of the trend, everything would be fair set for the Northern Rhône. Only a minority of the wines from recent vintages have enough alcohol to disturb me, but if conditions become even warmer, there is a risk that higher alcohol and lower acidity will change the style.

Two tiny appellations at the very southern tip of the northern Rhône, Brézème and St. Julian en Saint Alban, offer surprisingly cool climate impressions of both northern and southern varieties. During the nineteenth century, Brézème had a reputation equal to Hermitage, but it never recovered from phylloxera. "The traditional style of Brézème—if you can say that because there was only one grower left by the 1950s-1960s—is to be light. Now some growers are going for a bigger style—we have 6 growers and half are traditional and half are going for late harvest and extraction," says Eric Texier, who has contributed to the recent revival. The climate is relatively cool, resulting from winds coming off the hills to the vineyards halfway down the slopes of limestone terroir: "Especially for whites, Brézème is one of the places in the northern Rhône where naturally you get good acidity and low alcohol with ripeness." Brézème has the traditional northern varieties, Syrah and Viognier, as well as southern varieties. St. Julian en Saint Alban also has some Grenache; in fact it's the northernmost planting of Grenache in France. The wines of both appellations give cool climate impressions.

Vintages

The first decade of the 2000s has shown extremes from the universal heat wave of 2003 to the floods of 2002 or high rainfall of 2008. The best recent vintage is 2015, followed by 2009 or 2010 (depending on personal stylistic preferences), then 2005. "2010 had a beautiful balance; 2009 was more powerful and attracted more attention, but the press always talks about extremes," says Alberic Mazoyer at Domaine Alain Voge. "2009 will be an easily under-stood vintage of liquid pleasure, 2010 is a more serious vintage," says Philippe Guigal.

2016	?	Good quality but small crop, especially in Hermitage where there was hail.
2015	***	A top vintage with potential for great wines in a ripe, rich style.
2014		Difficulties in reaching ripeness for black grapes make this a year to approach cautiously. Rain around harvest was a problem.
2013	*	Decent, but not a great year, with an unusually late harvest compensating for difficulties during the growing season.
2012	**	Michel Chapoutier describes the vintage as "pure classicism," which means elegant fruits retaining freshness.
2011	*	Warm but not especially sunny; good but not as classic as 2010 or as ripe as 2009, with some dilution resulting from rain in September.

continued on next page

2010	***	Classic vintage giving textbook Syrah, fresh with good tension, widely regarded as having perfect balance and offering longevity.
2009	***	The vintage received widespread acclaim for its sheer ripeness: the wines are very appealing.
2008		Vintage was spoiled by high rainfall in the summer. Some top cuvées were not produced.
2007	*	Late start to the season was followed by cool conditions, but the vintage was rescued by a warm September: overall good rather than great.
2006	*	Warm September rescued the vintage from a mixed August and this is considered a good vintage for drinking before the 2005s.
2005	***	Considered the best year since 1990 in both north and south, giving wines with concentration and real longevity.
2004		Not many wines of interest today surviving in either north or south.
2003	*	Too hot everywhere: north better than south, but both questionable today.
2002		Poor all over southern France because of extensive floods.

Visiting the Region

The Northern Rhône is so extended that it really needs to be divided into two parts for visits.

Vienne is the obvious base for visiting Côte Rôtie, which is within just a few minutes drive, as well as Condrieu, Château Grillet, and the northern parts of St. Joseph (Chavanay and Malleval).

Tain l'Hermitage, or Tournon sur Rhône just across the river, are good bases for visiting Hermitage (which looms directly above the town of Tain l'Hermitage, where several producers have tasting rooms), as well as Crozes-Hermitage, and the southern part of St. Joseph (including Mauves where several producers are located), and Cornas and

St. Péray. A little farther south, Valance is a larger town within easy reach of many of the vineyards.

Except for St. Joseph, where it's a good idea to group producers by towns, it's easy to visits several producers in any one appellation in a day. The Northern Rhône is a mix with regards to interest in tourism: a few producers have tastings rooms that are open to visitors, especially around Côte Rôtie and Hermitage, but many do require appointments.

A visit will usually comprise a tasting and sometimes a tour of the facilities. Many producers have wines from more than one appellation, and single vineyard wines are becoming more common, so a tasting is likely to include around half a dozen different wines; usually it lasts about an hour.

Maps

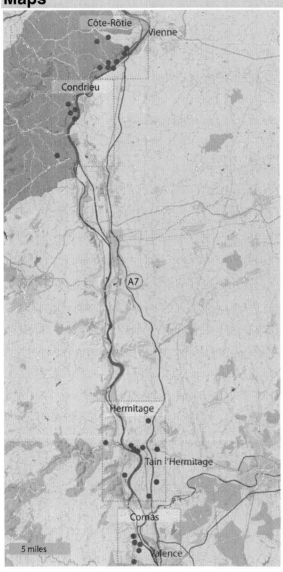

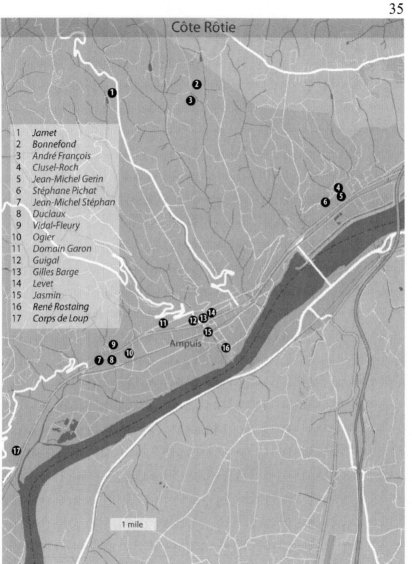

Côte Rôtie

1 Jamet
2 Bonnefond
3 André François
4 Clusel-Roch
5 Jean-Michel Gerin
6 Stéphane Pichat
7 Jean-Michel Stéphan
8 Duclaux
9 Vidal-Fleury
10 Ogier
11 Domain Garon
12 Guigal
13 Gilles Barge
14 Levet
15 Jasmin
16 René Rostaing
17 Corps de Loup

Ampuis

1 mile

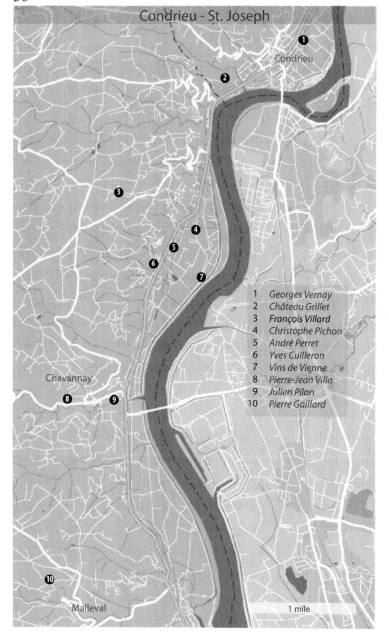

Condrieu - St. Joseph

Condrieu

1   Georges Vernay
2   Château Grillet
3   François Villard
4   Christophe Pichon
5   André Perret
6   Yves Cuilleron
7   Vins de Vienne
8   Pierre-Jean Villa
9   Julien Pilon
10 Pierre Gaillard

Chavannay

Malleval

1 mile

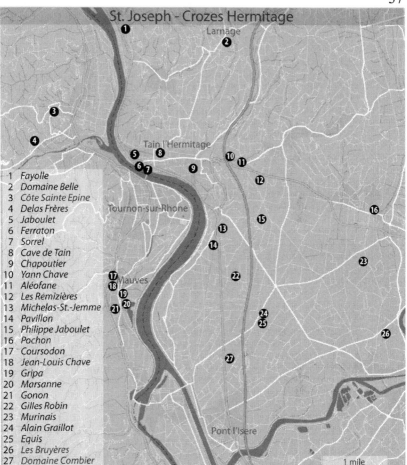

St. Joseph - Crozes Hermitage

1 Fayolle
2 Domaine Belle
3 Côte Sainte Epine
4 Delas Frères
5 Jaboulet
6 Ferraton
7 Sorrel
8 Cave de Tain
9 Chapoutier
10 Yann Chave
11 Aléofane
12 Les Remizières
13 Michelas-St.-Jemme
14 Pavillon
15 Philippe Jaboulet
16 Pochon
17 Coursodon
18 Jean-Louis Chave
19 Gripa
20 Marsanne
21 Gonon
22 Gilles Robin
23 Murinais
24 Alain Graillot
25 Equis
26 Les Bruyères
27 Domaine Combier

1 mile

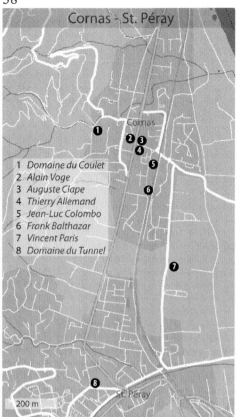

Cornas - St. Péray

1 Domaine du Coulet
2 Alain Voge
3 Auguste Clape
4 Thierry Allemand
5 Jean-Luc Colombo
6 Frank Balthazar
7 Vincent Paris
8 Domaine du Tunnel

Cornas

St. Péray

200 m

Profiles of Estates

Ratings	
****	Sui generis, standing out above everything else in the appellation
***	Excellent producers defining the very best of the appellation
**	Top producers whose wines typify the appellation
*	Very good producers making wines of character that rarely disappoint

Symbols

 Address

 Phone

 Person to contact

@ *Email*

⊕ *Website*

 Principal AOP

 Red *White   Reference wines*

 Grower-producer

 Negociant (or purchases grapes)

 Sustainable viticulture

 Organic

 Biodynamic

 Tasting room with especially warm welcome

 Tastings/visits possible

 By appointment only

 No visits

 Sales directly at producer

 No direct sales

ha=estate vineyards; bottles=annual production

Domaine Franck Balthazar *

 8 rue-des-Violettes, 07130 Cornas

 (33) 06 20 05 41 79

 Franck Balthazar

@ balthazar.franck@akeonet.com

Cornas

Cornas, Chaillot

 4 ha; 15,000 bottles

This must surely be the smallest domain I visited in the Rhône. It started with 1.2 ha in 1931, and since Franck Balthazar took over from his father, René, in 2002, he has tripled it. Franck does all the work in the vineyards himself. The wine is made in a small cellar with a dirt floor round the back of the church in the village.

The domain consists of three parcels in Cornas, Chaillot (1.7 ha), Mazards (0.4 ha), and Legre (1.7 ha), and also some recently planted vines in St. Péray. In 2011 there was a bottling under the Côtes du Rhône label from the young vines, which were very productive that year. Usually the Casimir bottling from Cornas comes from the young vines in the plot at Legre, which Franck replanted; it's warm, round, and nutty. At the other extreme, the Chaillot bottling comes from old vines replanted at the end of the nineteenth century just after phylloxera (some of this holding was inherited from Franck's uncle, Noël Verset); this makes an earthier, stonier, impression, with the intense, brooding black fruits of old vines.

The objective here is "to make wines with purity of fruit, not technological wines. I don't want any aggressivité in my tannins," Franck says. Everything is matured in old demi-muids. For all the intention to maintain tradition, the well-delineated fruits give an impression of precision, with tannins certainly tamed. The older vines offer a more concentrated impression than the young vines, but the same purity of style shows through.

Domaine Belle ★★

510 rue de la Croix Les Marsuriaux, 26600 Larnage

0)4 75 08 24 58

Philippe Belle

contact@domainebelle.com

www.domainebelle.com

Crozes-Hermitage

Crozes-Hermitage, Cuvée Louis Belle

Crozes-Hermitage, Terres Blanches

26 ha; 80,000 bottles

Up in the hills of Larnage at about 100m elevation in the heart of the original Crozes Hermitage appellation, Domaine Belle occupies a utilitarian building surrounded by vineyards. The domain has expanded significantly in Crozes Hermitage, where it's still possible to buy land. "It's impossible in Hermitage," Philippe Belle says.

The focus is decidedly on terroir. "We have always vinified by terroir. Why? Because we have very specific terroir, the only one here of white clay. Each terroir has its specificity and it's necessary to adapt to it. The white clay of Larnage is known for bringing freshness," says Philippe.

If I had to choose a single word to describe the wines of Domaine Belle, it would be finesse. At all levels the wines show precision, increasing as you go from Crozes Hermitage to St. Joseph to Hermitage, but the refined style is always evident.

The three cuvées from Crozes Hermitage make the case most forcefully: from the plain of Chassis, Les Pierelles is the most fruity; Cuvée Louis Belle from white clay terroir around the winery in Larnage has a fresh impression; and Roche Pierre from granitic terroir is taut.

Coming from the heart of St. Joseph, between Tournon and Mauves, the St. Joseph is more elegant yet; and with the Hermitage you reach a true vin de garde, with long keeping power, but also elegance.

These are textbook demonstrations of the effects of terroir on Syrah. There are also excellent whites from Crozes Hermitage and Hermitage.

Maison Chapoutier Vins Fins *

 18 Av Dr Paul Durand, 26600 Tain L'Hermitage

 (33) 04 75 08 28 65

 Michel Chapoutier

 chapoutier@chapoutier.com

 www.chapoutier.com

 Hermitage

St. Joseph, Les Granits

179 ha; 330,000 bottles

I left Chapoutier feeling slightly confused as to why I felt they might have lost their way. On previous visits, the wines were interesting all across the range. Now they seem more to be going through the motions. Chapoutier is both a large grower, with vineyards all across the Northern Rhône (the firm is the single largest owner of Hermitage), and a major negociant business handling wines from the entire Rhône.

Chapoutier is a major believer in single vineyard bottlings, and it's always been true that with Hermitage, the single vineyard wines are vastly more interesting than the blended cuvée, Monier de la Sizeranne; but the most recent vintages of Sizeranne seem somewhat rustic, which should never be the case for Hermitage. Chapoutier's top vineyard in St. Joseph, Les Granits, has in the past has produced some splendid wines, both red and white, almost worthy of Hermitage, but recent vintages seem lacking in character.

This is against a background of real interest in viticulture, with Chapoutier perhaps qualifying as the largest producer in France to be biodynamic, but I cannot find interest in the generic wines, or real conviction in the single vineyard wines, in the present releases. Perhaps expansion has been too rapid (Chapoutier now has interests elsewhere in France, and also in Portugal and Australia). The tasting room in the old headquarters in Tain l'Hermitage is thronged with visitors, although most wines now are made in a large modern facility away from the town.

Domaine Jean-Louis Chave ★★★★

37 Avenue de Saint Joseph, 07300 Mauves

(33) 04 75 08 24 63

Jean-Louis Chave

domainejlchave@hotmail.com

St. Joseph

Hermitage

27 ha; 45,000 bottles

The entrance to the most famous domain of Hermitage is quite deceptive, just a simple front door with a plate saying Gérard Chave on what appears to be an ordinary residence in the main street of Mauves. The doorway opens into a courtyard surrounded by winery buildings, with a rabbit warren of old cellars underneath. A new vinification cellar was built in 2014, with new vats that allow for softer treatment.

Jean-Louis Chave is widely acknowledged as a master of assemblage, and his Hermitage comes from a blend of plots on the hill that changes according to the year. The plots in Hermitage account for about half the domain. Wines from each plot are matured separately, in old barriques, with less than 20% new oak, until assemblage after about eighteen months..

The red is one of the longest-lived wines of Hermitage, and the white is equally fine. Some years there is also a limited bottling of Cuvée Cathelin, representing an alternative assemblage. In fat years this may perpetuate the tradition of Hermitage for strong structure more forcefully than the regular bottling. The white is mostly barrel-fermented and matured in oak, but a small part is kept in cuve. "It's a rich wine, based on glycerol," Jean-Louis says. He does not believe in the current trend for making white Rhône in a sparse, tighter style.

There is now St. Joseph from an old family vineyard that's being re-planted at Lemps, and the Clos de l'Arbalestrier, close to the cellars in Mauves, was purchased in 2009. Under the negociant label of JL Chave selections, there is a St. Joseph (Offerus), and also a characterful Crozes Hermitage (Silène). Vineyards are maintained by replacing vines individually as necessary by selection massale. "The grape is a vector for the soil to express itself. What I want is that what comes from Rocoule goes back to Rocoule," says Jean-Louis.

Domaine Clape ***

146 *Avenue du Colonel Rousset, 07130 Cornas*

(33) 04 75 40 33 64

Pierre & Olivier Clape

pierre.clape@wanadoo.fr

Cornas

Cornas

9 ha; 35,000 bottles

The domain was created when Auguste Clape left the Languedoc after the riots of 1907 and began to buy land in Cornas. Winemaker Olivier Clape is the third generation to produce wine under the domain name; his grandfather started bottling in 1955, his father Pierre-Marie took over, and then Olivier followed. Most of the vineyards are behind the village of Cornas, "not too high up," and there are also small plots in St. Péray and the Côtes du Rhône.

This is a traditional domain, with vinification in concrete tanks, and maturation in old foudres for 22-24 months. "The main difference between my father and grandfather was the date of picking," says Olivier, "and my father had lower yields. We don't want to have too much acidity because we keep 100% stems, so we pick a bit late."

There are two cuvées from Cornas. Introduced in 1998, Renaissance comes from young vines: young here means half from 12-16 years, giving yields of 36-38 hl/ha, the other half from 25-year-old vines on a south-facing site that is one of the warmest in Cornas. The traditional cuvée, labeled only with the appellation name, comes from older vines with lower yields, at 26-32 hl/ha. Tasting barrel samples from the various plots that go into the Cornas, there is a clear increase in aromatic complexity from 35-year-old vines to 80-year-old vines. The assembled Cornas is a vin de garde; give it sufficient time and you will see what Cornas is all about. The domain remains the reference point for Cornas.

Maison Clusel Roch

CÔTE-RÔTIE
APPELLATION CÔTE-RÔTIE CONTRÔLÉE

Clusel-Roch

2009

○ 15 Route du Lacat, 69420 Ampuis

📞 (33) 04 74 56 15 95

Guillaume Clusel

@ contact@domaine-clusel-roch.fr

🌐 www.domaine-clusel-roch.fr

⬤ Côte Rôtie

🍾 Côte Rôtie, Viallière

11 ha; 50,000 bottles

The winery is in what appears to be a modest house in a residential area. The principal production is Côte Rôtie, and there is also a little Condrieu. There are 5 ha in Côte Rôtie and 1 ha in Condrieu. Recently 2.5 ha were acquired in the Coteaux du Lyonnais (located north of Côte Rôtie), where plantings are Gamay and the wine is similar to Beaujolais.

From the several parcels in Côte Rôtie there are four cuvées: one general blend, one from young vines (La Petite Feuille), and two lieu-dits. There is partial destemming (0-50% depending on the year), stainless steel fermentation, pump-over and pump-down, 20-30 days' total maceration, and two years in barrique, with a little new oak but not too much (less than 20%). The Côte Rôties are 100% Syrah except for the classic (general) bottling which has a little Viognier. The old vines are perpetuated by selection massale, and Guillaume Clusel has been involved in a project to propagate old Serine vines.

The measure of the house is subtlety of approach. La Petite Feuille and the Côte Rôtie blend are not as interesting as the bottlings from the lieu-dits, Les Grandes Places and Les Vallières. Guillaume attributes the subtlety of the wines to time of harvesting. "We harvest just at maturity without sur-maturity," he says. The Condrieu shows equal subtlety, a fine demonstration that Viognier does not have to be taken to excess. The Gamays from the Coteaux du Lyonnais are good, but not exceptional.

Domaine Jean-Luc Colombo **

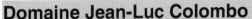

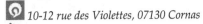 10-12 rue des Violettes, 07130 Cornas

 (33) 04 75 84 17 10

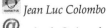 Jean Luc Colombo

 @ colombo@vinscolombo.fr

 www.vinscolombo.fr

 Cornas

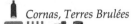 Cornas, Terres Brulées

12 ha; 100,000 bottles

Jean-Luc Colombo was regarded as a young Turk, if not a revolutionary, when he started to buy land on the higher Cornas slopes in the 1980s, not to mention introducing new oak into his cuvées. The 12 ha of estate vineyards in Cornas are broken up into 25 different parcels. The modernist approach extends to complete destemming—"Syrah is a very tannic variety," says Laure Colombo. "When my parents were criticized for making more sophisticated wine, people would say, this wine is not typical," she recollects. But Jean-Luc has won the argument as his approach is now common in Cornas.

The bulk of production is through a negociant business, with around thirty wines, the biggest line being the Côtes du Rhône. The style of the negociant wines is direct and fruity: these are well made wines for immediate consumption, but they do not have the interest of the wines from the estate vineyards, especially when you move to single vineyard cuvées.

These are modern wines in the sense that the fruit clearly comes first, but I would not accuse Jean-Luc, at least not today, of being a modernist in the sense that the wines show excess new oak: the oak is judicious, just showing on the youngest vintages, but well integrated after, say, five years. If the wines do not always rise to the heights that you would really like to see, they are true to type in reflecting vintage, with the single-parcel 2006 Cornas Les Ruchets, for example, giving a more reserved impression than the more exuberant 2009.

Domaine Combier **

CROZES-HERMITAGE
APPELLATION CROZES-HERMITAGE CONTRÔLÉE

DOMAINE COMBIER
2009

12.5% vol   Mis en bouteille au domaine   750 ml
Pont de l'Isère 26600 Tain l'Hermitage « F »
Produce of France · Contient des sulfites

Clos des Grives

📍 *1440 route de Lyon, 26600 Pont-de-l'Isère*

📞 *04 75 84 61 56*

👤 *Laurent Combier*

@ *contact@domaine-combier.fr*

🌐 *www.domaine-combier.com*

⚫ *Crozes-Hermitage*

🚶 🍶 🍇 🍾

30 ha; 150,000 bottles

Maurice Combier came to Pont de l'Isère to grow apricots and other fruit in 1962, and became known as Maurice Le Fou (Crazy Maurice) when he turned to organic agriculture in the 1970s. Grapes from the domain were sold to the cooperative. His son Laurent studied viticulture and joined the domain in 1989. At that point the estate had 5 ha of vines and 15 ha of peaches and apricots. Laurent moved the domain into viticulture, built a cave, and started to produce wine.

Most of the vineyards are around Pont de l'Isère (in the Crozes Hermitage AOP about four miles south of Hermitage); there are also smaller holdings across the river in St. Joseph. Cuvée Laurent Combier is an introductory blend that comes from rented vineyards. Cap Nord is a new line, started in 2010, from parcels in the north of the Crozes Hermitage and St. Joseph appellations.

The Domaine Combier Crozes Hermitage cuvées are blends from several estate parcels in the vicinity of Pont de l'Isère. The top cuvées come from the Clos des Grives, a 9.5 ha vineyard just next to Alain Graillot's estate; this has the oldest vines of the domain, 4 ha that were planted in 1952. The red is pure Syrah, the white is 95% Roussanne. Grapes are destemmed and fermented in stainless steel; then they are matured in cuve for Cuvée Laurent Combier, in old barriques for the domain, and in barriques with about a quarter new oak for Clos des Grives. Laurent Combier also is a partner in a domain (Trio Infernal) in Priorat (Spain).

Cave Yves Cuilleron **

Rn 86 Verlieu 42140 Chavanay

(33) 04 74 87 02 37

Yves Cuilleron

ycuiller@terre-net.fr

www.cuilleron.com

Condrieu

Côte Rôtie, Bassenon

St. Joseph, Saint Pierre

56 ha; 350,000 bottles

This family domain was created by Yves's grandfather when he planted vines in 1920. He started in bottling in 1947. When Yves took over the domain in 1987, there were 4 ha; today vineyards have expanded considerably from the original holdings in St. Joseph and Condrieu to Côte Rôtie, Cornas, and St. Péray. "Now it is difficult to buy land, but when I started there was plenty of land for sale," Yves says. The modern tasting room just off the main road is thronged with visitors. With a reputation in the region for producing wines in a more modern style, Yves is also one of the entrepreneurs behind the Vins de Vienne.

Cuilleron produces 25 different wines. "In each appellation there are several cuvées. You can make cuvées by lieu-dit or by style. I prefer the second because many parcels are very broken up, and very small, so I make cuvées de style, some more fruity, some more structured coming from an assemblage of parcels with the same character."

All plots are vinified separately. The AOP wines are matured in barriques. There's been some retreat on the amount of new oak, which today is less than 20% except for the vins de garde. Whites have 9 months élevage and reds have 18 months. It's not surprising that with 25 different cuvées there should be some variety, and style here depends on the level. The introductory cuvées from each appellation tend to be fruity; the more advanced show more of a mixture of influences with savory notes on nose and palate.

Maison Delas Frères ✸✸

Allée de L'Olivet, 07304 Saint Jean de Muzols

(33) 04 75 08 60 30

Michel & Jean-François Gaillard

france@delas.com

www.delas.com

St. Joseph

St. Joseph, François de Tournon

Condrieu, Clos Boucher

29 ha; 1,500,000 bottles

Delas was founded as a negociant of Hermitage in 1834, and after its acquisition by Champagne Deutz in 1977, came under the ownership of Champagne Roederer when Roederer acquired Deutz in 1993. It presently functions out of a utilitarian building constructed fifteen years ago across the road from the original site, just under the hill of Saint Epine, which is the top cuvée from St. Joseph. The estate vineyards break down into 10 ha in Hermitage (including 8 ha in Les Bessards), 17 ha in Crozes Hermitage, and 2 ha in St. Joseph.

About half of production comes from the estate vineyards; the other half is a negociant business based on purchased grapes. Many of the domain bottlings are identified as Domaine des Tourettes. Production is largely red, with only about 10% white.

The style here tends towards a silky refinement, running through the best reds from Crozes Hermitage, St. Joseph, and Hermitage. Even at the lower levels, the wines are finely balanced, which is to say following the traditions of the region as opposed to pandering to a style for jammy fruits. They are all recognizably from the Northern Rhône, with typicity of the individual appellation, in which freshness is balanced by a sheen of glycerin in the house style.

Delas also has a range of wines from the Southern Rhône; richer but less refined, these typify the difference between south and the north. The wines are always reliable, although of course the top cuvées from the better appellations have the most interest.

Maison Michel Ferraton Père & Fils   **

🌀 13 rue Maurice de La Sizeranne, 26600 Tain L'Hermitage

📞 (33) 04 75 08 59 51

👤 Michel Ferraton

@ ferraton@ferraton.fr

🌐 www.ferraton.fr

⬤ Hermitage

🍾 Hermitage, Les Miaux

St. Joseph, La Source

13 ha; 350,000 bottles

The domain started in 1998 when Michel Ferraton left Chapoutier. After he had a serious accident in 2007, the firm was bought by Chapoutier, although it continues to run independently. Chapoutier does have an influence however: Ferraton has the same belief in emphasizing bottlings of individual *climats* rather than a single assemblage, and also has biodynamic vineyards in Hermitage, Crozes Hermitage, and St. Joseph.

"Our philosophy is to express the different terroirs found in the Northern Rhône. We want to show the different typicities we find in St. Joseph, the difference between granite and other soils, or in Cornas the difference between elevations," says manager Olivier Goni. There are five different cuvées from Hermitage: two are from assemblage of various plots, and the others come from Méal, Dionnières, and a blend of Méal and Dionnières; there are two cuvées from each of the other appellations.

There is also a negociant business, principally for wines from the Southern Rhône, but also including Côte Rôtie, and this is much larger than the production of estate wines. The greatest part of the business is the negociant wine from Côtes du Rhône and Crozes Hermitage.

The style is towards freshness rather than exuberance; "We look for discretion and elegance," says Olivier. The reds are relatively restrained, and the whites fulfill the aim of maintaining freshness; there is good weight on the palate, but they are wines to drink in five years rather than hold for ten.

Domaine Pierre Gaillard **

Lieu Dit Chez Favier, 42520 Malleval

(33) 04 74 87 13 10

Pierre Gaillard

famille@gaillard.vin

www.gaillard.vin

St. Joseph

St. Joseph, Les Pierres

25 ha; 125,000 bottles

There's a distinctly thoughtful air at this domain, tucked away on the plateau above the medieval village of Malleval. Pierre Gaillard has an interest in the old Roman wines—each year he makes a wine in an amphora using different experimental procedures—and he was instrumental in reviving the old vineyards at Seyssuel when he started the Vins de Vienne.

Although committed to preserving the character of the region, in winemaking he is a modernist, using around 20% new oak for his St. Joseph and Côte Rôtie. All wines are matured in barriques but there is no new oak for the whites, "Because the whites have minerality but not acidity."

Pierre's first vineyard showed typical lateral thinking. "The first land I bought was in Chavanay, I wanted to make a Viognier, but there was no land in Condrieu. This was probably not included in Condrieu because it is east-facing, but I heard it had made good Viognier before."

There's an impressive range of wines here, with 48 cuvées altogether, made to a high standard with each typical of its appellation, from the round Côte Rôtie, to the fresh St. Joseph, and the slightly stern Cornas. Wines from Pierre's daughter Jeanne are also available under the Gaillard name, and Pierre has expanded into Faugères (Domaine Cottebrun) and Banyuls (Domaine Madeloc), "Just for pleasure, around here it is all Syrah, I wanted the experience of other varieties. Here we could not expand. My passion is to understand terroir."

Domaine Jean-Michel Gerin **

19 rue de Montmain, Vérenay, 69420 Ampuis

(33) 04 74 56 16 56

Jean-Michel Gerin

info@domaine-gerin.fr

www.domaine-gerin.fr

Côte Rôtie

Côte Rôtie, Le Seigneur

12 ha; 100,000 bottles

The family has been involved in wine in Ampuis for six generations, but Jean-Michel created the domain in 1983 with one small parcel on Côte Rôtie; it has been expanding ever since. His sons Michaël et Alexis are now involved.

The original vineyard holdings were all close to Ampuis, with 7 ha in a dozen separate plots in Côte Rôtie and another 2 ha in Condrieu. The major Côte Rôtie, Champin le Seigneur, is an assemblage from all the sites, but mostly from the Côte Brune, and includes 10% Viognier. In addition there are single vineyard bottlings from the *climats* Grandes Places (since 1988), which is considered Gerin's top wine, La Landonne (since 1996), and La Viallière (planted only in 2003, with the first vintage in 2009). These are all exclusively Syrah. Another site on Côte Rôtie, Les Lezards, is presently being planted. There is a single Condrieu, La Loye. More recently, a St. Joseph red has been added, together with Syrah and Viognier under the IGP Collines Rhodaniennes.

The style here is modern, with destemming, and maturation in barriques including lots of new oak for 18 months. Grandes Places and La Landonne use 100% new barriques, La Viallière uses 100% new demi-muids, and other wines use varying proportions. There is frequent battonage. The Condrieu uses a mix of stainless steel and one-year barriques. (There's also a collaborative venture with two other producers from southern France to make wine at a 6 ha domain in Priorat, Spain.)

Domaine Alain Graillot ★★

🍇 *105 chemin des Chenes Verts, Pont de l'Isère, 26600*

📞 *(33) 04 75 84 67 52*

CONTACTS *Maxime Graillot*

@ contact@domainegraillot.com

St. Joseph

St. Joseph

21 ha; 100,000 bottles

Alain Graillot is one of the new generation who came into winemaking in search of something different from the corporate world. He established his domain in Crozes Hermitage in 1985. Self taught as a winemaker since there was no wine in the family background, he rapidly acquired a reputation for his thoughtful approach, which maintains tradition, for example by manual harvesting rather than the mechanization that is common in Crozes Hermitage.

The heart of the domain consists of vineyards on the Plain de Chassis in the southern part of Crozes Hermitage, more or less centered on the cellars, which are located just outside the town of Pont de l'Isère between Tain l'Hermitage and Valence. In addition, there is a small vineyard at Larnage in the hills to the north of Crozes Hermitage, on granite terroir, and also two tiny parcels in St. Joseph. The top cuvée is a barrel selection from Crozes Hermitage, made only in top years, La Guiraude. Production is mostly red, but the white Crozes Hermitage, a blend of 80% Marsanne with 20% Roussanne, has acquired a high reputation. Wines are aged in 1- to 3-year-old barriques.

The wines have a reputation for moderation, which is a contrast with Alain's more recent involvement with winemaking elsewhere, notably with wines from Australia and Morocco now associated with his name. Since 2008, the wines at Alain Graillot have been made by his son Maxime, who also makes wines at his own domain, Domaine des Lises, where he also functions as a negociant under the name of Équis (see mini-profile).

Château Grillet **

⊙ *42410 Vérin*

📞 *(33) 04 74 59 51 56*

CONTACT US *Alessandro Noli*

@ *contact@chateau-grillet.com*

⊕ *chateau-grillet.com*

◉ *Château Grillet*

🚫 ⚔ 🍇

4 ha; 8,000 bottles

A monopole, Château Grillet is one of the smallest AOPs in France, occupying an amphitheater overlooking the Rhône, with steeply terraced vineyards running from 150m up to 200m that form an enclave surrounded by Condrieu. Owned by the Neyret-Gachet family from 1827 to 2011, it was a benchmark for Viognier (the only grape grown), although after the planted area was expanded from 1.7 ha to 3.5 ha during the 1970s-1980s, the style was felt to be a little tired. In 2004, Denis Dubourdieu, who was largely responsible for resurrecting white wine production in Bordeaux, was brought in as a consultant, and the style became fresher.

Things changed entirely when Château Grillet was sold to M. Pinault (owner of Château Latour). Changes in the vineyard led to a dramatic drop in yields. A new cellar was installed in 2012, with many small stainless steel tanks, so each plot can be fermented separately. Wines are aged in barriques with only a little new oak. With the intention of restoring Grillet to its former glory, a second wine was introduced under the Côtes du Rhone appellation; called Pontcin, it is declassified from Château Grillet and sells for about a quarter of the price of the grand vin. Château Grillet is known for its minerality; this is less evident in Pontcin, which tends more to the floral notes associated with Condrieu

Maison Guigal ***

 Château d'Ampuis, 69420 Ampuis

 (33) 04 74 56 10 22

 Philippe Guigal

 contact@guigal.com

 www.guigal.com

 Côte Rôtie

 Côte Rôtie, Château d'Ampuis

Crozes Hermitage

128 ha; 8,000,000 bottles

The entire atmosphere in the Northern Rhône changed when Marcel Guigal introduced single vineyard cuvées from Côte Rôtie in the 1970s. His father had founded Maison Guigal in 1946; today his son Philippe has taken over as chief winemaker. Estate vineyards now extend all over the Northern Rhône, with top sites in Hermitage and St. Joseph coming from the purchase of the old Grippat estate, adding the Vigne de l'Hospice (St. Joseph) and Ex Voto (Hermitage) to the La Landonne, La Mouline, and La Turque single vineyard cuvées from Côte Rôtie.

The single vineyard cuvées are certainly powerful and spicy, but tannins are tamed by the fruits, and new oak is not overwhelming. There is also an homage to tradition here in the form of the Brune et Blonde cuvée (a blend from the different areas of Côte Rôtie) and the Château d'Ampuis (a selection of the best lots from various terroirs).

With a current production of 6.5 million bottles, Guigal is the most important negociant in the Northern Rhône, although the majority of the negociant business, including 3.5 million bottles of Côtes du Rhône, comes from the Southern Rhône. Guigal has also purchased Vidal Fleury (which remains independently run), where Étienne Guigal worked before founding Maison Guigal. An expansion into the top area of the Southern Rhône came with the acquisition in 2017 of the 50 ha Domaine de Nalys, one of the oldest estates in Châteauneuf du Pape.

All this has been accomplished while retaining a concern for quality and character. For example, "I've never been a big fan of Grenache Blanc," says Philippe. "Thirty years ago my dad was struggling to get Viognier, it was only 5% then, but today the white Côtes du Rhône is 60% Viognier. It took thirty years, but we achieved it." A splendid new headquarters has been constructed across the road, connected to the original winery by a tunnel. (The winery covers 3 ha.) Guigal has the rare distinction of being a quality leader in both estate and negociant wines.

Domaines Paul Jaboulet Aîné ★★

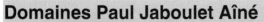

25 Place du Taurobole, 26600 Tain l'Hermitage

(33) 04 75 84 68 93

Caroline Frey

@ info@jaboulet.com

www.jaboulet.com

Hermitage

St. Joseph, Domaine de la Croix de Vigne

Hermitage, Chevalier de Sterimberg

115 ha; 200,000 bottles

"We are the smallest of the big negociants," says winemaker Ralph Garcin. Jaboulet is a great old name, famous from the mid-twentieth century for its blended Hermitage, La Chapelle, but quality had slipped by the time the Frey family (of Château La Lagune in the Médoc) took it over in 2006. (It has never been clear why the estate was sold, since seven members of the Jaboulet family were still active in it. Philippe Jaboulet went on to found his own domain: see mini-profile.) The new owners have started a forceful expansion, increasing estate vineyards from the 80 ha at the time of take-over, adding vineyards in Châteauneuf-du-Pape as well as in the Northern Rhône.

"For every appellation in the Rhône we have a minimum of two wines, one from the estate and one from the negociant. We look for more consistency in the negociant line," says Ralph. Differences between wines here are due to intrinsic character, as fermentation and élevage are similar for the whole range; new oak is presently around 20% but will decrease to about 15%. "We are looking for freshness and elegance even if it is a warm spot like Châteauneuf-du-Pape," Ralph says

La Chapelle remains the flagship. Quality slipped through the nineties, partly because volume increased, reaching 9,000 cases by 2000. A second wine, La Petite Chapelle, was introduced in in 2001 to decrease quantity, but the real recovery began after the sale in 2006. "La Chapelle had to become what it used to be. When we took over, we decided to keep Petite Chapelle and make it more fruit-driven, more approachable young. It's a second wine, but it's not a simple declassification—sometimes some lots are shared between the wines," explains Ralph Garcin.

I was impressed with the progress when I tasted a range of domain wines from recent vintages. La Chapelle is good once again (although I have my doubts about whether Petit Chapelle really represents Hermitage), the white Chevalier de Sterimberg is right on form, and there are interesting wines from Crozes Hermitage, St. Joseph, and Condrieu. I was less certain about the Châteauneuf-du-Pape (but I often have reservations about Southern Rhône wines from Northern Rhône producers).

Domaine Jamet 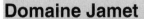 **

  4600 *Route du Recru "Le Vallin" 69420 Ampuis*

 (33) 04 74 56 12 57

 Corinne, Jean-Paul & Loïc Jamet

 domainejamet@wanadoo.fr

 Côte Rôtie

14 ha; 75,000 bottles

Until the eighties, the family business was polyculture, mostly concentrating on growing apricots. Once the focus switched to grapes, Joseph Jamet became regarded as one of the most traditional producers in the appellation, and the style was continued when he retired in 1991 and his sons Jean-Paul and Jean Luc took over.

Two thirds of Jamet's vineyards are in Côte Rôtie, spread around 26 different parcels in a variety of lieu-dits, three quarters in Côte Brune and a quarter in Côte Blonde. Vines range from 25 to 50 years old; there is only Syrah. Some parcels are vinified and aged separately, while others are blended. Some are destemmed while others are not; there are significant differences from year to year. Wines are matured in a mixture of barriques and demi-muids, with a trend towards increasing the proportion of demi-muids in recent years. New oak is around 20%.

The philosophy here is to represent the domain with one wine; "My philosophy, it's assemblage," says Jean-Paul. "I don't like to focus on a wine, a parcel, or a year," but there is a cuvée, Côte Brune, made from a single 0.5 ha parcel in the best years. In fact, this was the sole production when Joseph Jamet started the domain; now it is only 5%. There are also both red and white Côtes du Rhône, from the one third of vineyards outside Côte Rôtie. However, as of 2013 the brothers have split, with Jean-Paul retaining the domain, and Jean-Luc creating a new domain based on the Lancement parcel in Côte Rôtie.

Domaine Jasmin **

 14, rue des Maraîchers 69420 Ampuis

📞 04 74 56 16 04

Patrick & Arelette Jasmin

@ jasmin.pa@wanadoo.fr

Côte Rôtie

Côte Rôtie

7.5 ha; 30,000 bottles

This typical small domain on Côte Rôtie, now in its fourth generation since Patrick Jasmin gave up cross-country motorcycling to take over from his father Robert in 1999, has 6 ha of eleven separate parcels spread over nine lieu-dits in Côte Rôtie, with terroirs of both schist and granite. Including some additional leased vineyards, the average vine age is over thirty years.

The vineyards are coplanted with 95% Syrah and 5% Viognier; the proportion of Viognier in the finished wine varies, depending on the vintage. Propagated by selection massale in the estate vineyards, the Syrah is the old Sérine selection. Parcels are vinified separately, the wine is racked into barriques for malolactic fermentation, and then all the wine goes into a single assemblage to make the unique Côte Rôtie, which is matured for two years in a mixture of barriques and demi-muids, with around a quarter new oak. In addition, there is a Syrah in IGP de Collines Rhodaniennes, which comes from 1.5 ha of vineyards below Côte Rôtie.

Robert Jasmin was known for his traditional approach (he was considered to be one of the holdouts for the old style, together with Auguste Clape and Joseph Jamet), but there has been some modernization in recent years, with de-stemming introduced and a saignée to concentrate the must. The style tends towards elegance rather than power, with freshness evident, even a touch lean at times, but with complex aromatics and oak not at all evident. This is tradition at its best.

Domaine Michel et Stéphane Ogier **

3 Chemin du Bac, 69420 Ampuis

(33) 04 74 56 10 75

Stéphane Ogier

sogier@domaine-ogier.fr

www.domaine-ogier.fr

Côte Rôtie

13 ha; 80,000 bottles

Michel Ogier sold his grapes to Chapoutier and Guigal until 1983, when he started to bottle his own wine from his tiny 3 ha vineyard in Côte Rôtie. His son Stéphane spent five years studying viticulture and oenology in Burgundy, and then returned home to join the domain in 1997. "That is why great Burgundy, along with Rhônes, are my preferred red wines," he says. One of his main objectives was to increase the estate to a more economic size, and he added vineyards in several lieu-dits in Côte Rôtie, and at La Rosine just above Côte Rôtie, as well as planting Syrah farther up the river at Seyssuel. His most recent acquisition was a hectare in Condrieu.

Renamed Domaine Michel & Stéphane Ogier, the domain now produces a variety of cuvées: Côte Rôtie is presently a blend from 10 parcels in the appellation; the IGP Collines Rhodaniennes comes from La Rosine; and the L'Âme de Soeur cuvée comes from Seyssuel. There are two prestige cuvées from Côte Rôtie, Lancement from Côte Blonde, and Belle Hélène, a selection from old vines that is aged exclusively in new oak. There is also a small negociant activity producing a Côtes du Rhône from Plan de Dieu (the area in the southern Rhône between Vacqueyras and Cairanne). Most production is red, but there is a Viognier from La Rosine, as well as the Condrieu. The style of the wines is modern (with about 30% new oak in the regular Côte Rôtie), and you might call the top cuvées very modern.

Domaine André Perret *

9 17, Verlieu, (RN 86), 42410 Chavanay

📞 (33) 04 74 87 24 74

André Perret

@ andre.perret@terre-net.fr

🌐 www.andreperret.com

Condrieu

St. Joseph, Les Grisières

Condrieu, Chéry

13 ha; 55,000 bottles

The Perret family were vignerons in Chassagne Montrachet until they relocated as a result of the second world war. André's father and grandfather cultivated fruits, and André abandoned a career as a biologist to start the domain by renting a vineyard in the Coteau de Chéry lieu-dit of Condrieu. Then he obtained a tiny area of his own vines from his uncle. Initially in 1983 the domain consisted of just 1 ha in Condrieu. It's been built up slowly since then, but remains a small domain today, with the winery in what looks like a residence just off the main road in Chavanay, although in fact a new cave was constructed in 1995.

Today the AOP vineyard holdings are split between St. Joseph and Condrieu, and there are also 2 ha planted within the IGP on the plain. Basically André plants Viognier in the warmest spots (to make Condrieu) and Syrah, Marsanne, or Roussanne elsewhere (to make St. Joseph). There are three Condrieus and three St. Josephs (one white and two red). The interest here is in terroir: "I'm a Burgundian, I respect terroir," André says of his bottlings from lieu-dits in Condrieu. The Coteau de Chéry, which is still the top cuvée, and the old vines Les Grisières bottling of a red St. Joseph, are the most interesting wines. The style is quite fine, and both the Condrieu and St. Joseph are good representations of the appellations. The white St. Joseph is an equal blend of Marsanne and Roussanne, and gets about 10% new oak. "It's not typical but the Roussanne makes the wine finer," André says.

Domaine des Remizières ⃰

1459 *Avenue du Vercors, 26600 Mercurol*

(33) 04 75 07 44 28

Philippe, Christophe, & Emilie Desmeure

contact@domaineremizieres.com

www.domaineremizieres.com

Crozes-Hermitage

Hermitage, Cuvée Emilie

36 ha; 160,000 bottles

This family domain (also known as Cave Desmeure) started with 4 ha in the late 1960s; originally Alphonse Desmeure sold half the wine to the cooperative and the other half to negociants, but domain bottling started in 1973. Philippe Desmeure took over in 1996 and was responsible for enlarging the estate; now he has been joined by his daughter Emilie. The first vineyards were in Crozes Hermitage, and then Hermitage and St. Joseph were added. Production is all from estate vineyards except for a Cornas made from purchased grapes. The operation is still expanding, as witnessed by the building materials and cranes everywhere when I visited.

The wines are all well made, but to my mind they seem to risk becoming superficial: it's difficult to get a feeling of character, or a personality behind them. Quite a bit of new oak is used (100% for the red Hermitage, 50% for the white). No white grapes are used in the red wines. "It's not needed any more," Emilie explains. The consistent house style shows something of an impression of glycerin on the palate, giving almost a sense of sweetness on the finish; this can verge on oppressive in the less expensive cuvées, but is more pleasing at the higher end where there is sufficient balancing structure. The top wines are named for the current generation: Cuvée Christophe is a red Crozes Hermitage from old vines on the slopes (whereas the entry level cuvée comes from the plain); the top red Hermitage is called Cuvée Emilie, as is the white Hermitage.

Domaine René Rostaing ★★★

⊙ *1 Petite Rue du Port, 69420 Ampuis*

✆ *René Rostaing*

@ *info@domainerostaing.com*

🌐 *www.domainerostaing.com*

◻ *Côte Rôtie*

🍾 *Côte Rôtie, Ampodium*

10 ha; 40,000 bottles

The modest premises consist of a purpose-built concrete facility with a cellar underground, off a small courtyard behind the family residence in Ampuis. Although the domain started with under a hectare in 1971, today the vineyards consist of 25 separate parcels in Côte Rôtie and Condrieu; there is also now a small domain in the Languedoc (Puech Noble). (Why expand into Languedoc? "For experience of other grape varieties and terroir. It's easy to buy land in Languedoc, here it's impossible.")

There are three cuvées from Côte Rôtie: Ampodium (the general bottling), La Landonne (from a 2 ha plot), and Côte Blonde, which is the best, but most tannic, wine. The mark of the house, for both Condrieu and Côte Rôtie, is subtlety. "When I describe my vinification, winemakers become very excited because they think I have a secret," René says, "but I have no secret. The only secret is no intervention. If you have too much intervention in vinification, you make a factory wine."

René uses a rotary fermenter, which in other hands might lead to too much extraction, and alcohol is usually no more than 13%. There is no destemming: this is a puzzle given the evident gracefulness and elegance of the wines. "If you respect the grape, it's not necessary to destem," is all René will say about it. Both barriques and demi-muids are used for aging, and there is a very little new oak. However it is achieved, the style is old school elegance rather than modern power.

Domaine Marc Sorrel ★★★

128 bis Ave Jean Jaures, Tain L'Hermitage, 26600

(33) 04 75 07 10 07

Marc Sorrel

contact@marcsorrel.fr

www.marcsorrel.fr

Hermitage

Hermitage, Les Rocoules

4 ha; 15,000 bottles

The domain was started in 1928 by Marc Sorrel's grandfather, Félix; grapes were sold to the cooperative until his son, Henri, started domain bottling in 1979. Marc took over in 1984. When Henri Sorrel died, the domain was divided between Marc and his brother, Jean-Michel (whose domain is called J.M.B. Sorrel). Marc subsequently acquired some plots in Crozes Hermitage, but this remains one of the smallest quality domains in the region; the key vineyard holding is the 2.5 ha in top sites on the hill of Hermitage.

There are two red and two white cuvées of Hermitage. The principal cuvées—just labeled with the appellation name—are blends from Les Plantiers and Les Greffieux. The prestige red cuvée is called Le Gréal, to reflect its origins in an assemblage from Le Méal and Les Greffieux, and includes 10% Marsanne. The prestige white cuvée comes from Les Rocoules. The red and white Crozes Hermitage both come from the hills around Larnage. The wines were uneven for the first few years after Marc took over, but have certainly bounced back since then.

The approach has been traditional. Everything is aged in oak (up to 24 months for the top cuvées); the whites are barrel-fermented. Only old oak was used until 2004, when new oak, generally up to a quarter, was introduced. The style has been riper since the 2000 vintage, when Marc switched to harvesting later. Both reds and whites offer fine examples of fruit purity. Most of the production is exported.

Domaine du Tunnel

*

Stéphane **ROBERT**

SAINT-JOSEPH

DOMAINE
DU TUNNEL

2010

🌐 *20 Rue de la République, 07130 Saint-Péray*

📞 *(33) 04 75 80 04 66*

Stéphane Robert

@ *domaine-du-tunnel@wanadoo.fr*

St. Péray

Cornas

8 ha; 35,000 bottles

It's unusual to find top domains headquartered in St. Péray, which has been painfully making the switch from sparkling to still wines, and has had some trouble establishing its identity, but this is where Stéphane Robert established his domain in 1994, after an apprenticeship with Jean-Louis Grippat in Tournon. (The name of the domain comes from an old railway tunnel that runs underneath.)

Starting with leased vineyards, Stéphane slowly built up the domain with his own holdings in Cornas, St. Joseph, and St. Péray. The largest holding is in Cornas, with parcels in fifteen different sites, including some vineyards from the old Marcel Juge domain, which added some very old vines to the portfolio. The St. Joseph comes from parcels in Tournon, Glun, and Mauves, in the heart of the original St. Joseph appellation. The St. Péray includes a varietal Roussanne bottling (somewhat of a contrast with the usual amorphous flavors of the appellation). As well as the appellation wine from Cornas (a blend from many parcels), there is the Cornas Vin Noir (a real vin de garde coming from vines that are around a hundred years old).

Stéphane's stated objective is to produce wine with intensity rather than oak flavors, so the wines are matured in old (4- to 6-year) barriques. The style is clean and modern in the sense that there's none of the animal notes that used to characterize Cornas, but traditional in the sense that the wines aren't overly influenced by oak.

Domaine Georges Vernay  **

 *1, Route Nationale, 69420 Condrieu*

 *(33) 04 74 56 81 81*

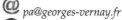 *Christine Vernay*

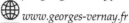 *pa@georges-vernay.fr*

 www.georges-vernay.fr

 *Condrieu*

 Condrieu, Terrasses de l'Empire

24 ha; 120,000 bottles

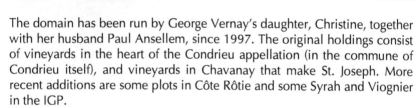

The domain has been run by George Vernay's daughter, Christine, together with her husband Paul Ansellem, since 1997. The original holdings consist of vineyards in the heart of the Condrieu appellation (in the commune of Condrieu itself), and vineyards in Chavanay that make St. Joseph. More recent additions are some plots in Côte Rôtie and some Syrah and Viognier in the IGP.

The domain has a high reputation for its Condrieus, which show a subtle, elegant style. There are three cuvées. The largest is Les Terrasses de l'Empire, which comes from the lieu-dits St. Agathe and La Caille. Chailles de l'Enfer is a smaller production, coming from La Caille, and is more reserved. Coteaux de Vernon is regarded as one of the defining cuvées for the appellation, coming from a 2 ha plot of old vines (50- to 80-year) on biotite (a type of granite); located in the center of the appellation, this is considered to be one of the best sites in Condrieu. This was the original vineyard holding when the domain was created.

All the wines are matured in barrique, with about one quarter new oak for the top cuvées. The Condrieus are barrel-fermented. The Côte Rôtie, Blonde du Seigneur, is softened with 5% Viognier. The two cuvées from St. Joseph are both relatively fruity and forward. There's also a Côtes du Rhône, Sainte Agathe, from vineyards near Condrieu, several IGP Syrah cuvées (Maison Rouge, Fleur de Mai, and De Mirbaudie) and an IGP Viognier. The domain is not particularly receptive to visits.

Maison Vidal-Fleury   *

48, Route de Lyon, 69420 Tupin et Semons. France

(33) 04 74 56 10 18

Guy Sartron du Jonchay

vidal-fleury@wanadoo.fr

www.vidal-fleury.com

Côte Rôtie

62 ha; 1,000,000 bottles

Founded in 1781, Vidal Fleury is one of the old-line negociants in the Northern Rhône. In fact, it's the oldest negociant still in business. Starting in Ampuis, it expanded into other regions of the Rhône in the 1920s. The wines had a good reputation until the late seventies (I remember some excellent Côte Rôties from the sixties), when they began to be regarded as dull, especially after Joseph Vidal died in 1976. By the 1980s Vidal-Fleury was in difficulties, until it was purchased by Marcel Guigal in 1984; his father had been the chef de cave until he left to establish Maison Guigal.

Vidal Fleury continues to run independently (although its best vineyards on Côte Rôtie, including La Turque, are now part of the Guigal portfolio). It has benefited from new investment since the takeover, including the construction in 2009 of a massive new winery in Ampuis, which the locals describe as looking like an ancient Egyptian temple. Vidal Fleury remains a sizeable negociant business (although only about 15% of the size of Guigal itself), making reliable wines from about twenty different appellations all over the Rhône. Packaging and style have been modernized.

"We saw an opportunity when we opened the new winery," says winemaker Guy Sarton du Jonchay. "We tried to make a wine that's more modern, more fruity." It's an open question whether the style is more modern than Guigal, but it is fair to say that Vidal Fleury does not rise to the same heights as Guigal.

Les Vins de Vienne

1 Zone d'Activité de Jassoux, 42410 Chavanay

(33) 04 74 85 04 52

Denis Chorot

contact@lesvinsdevienne.fr

www.vinsdevienne.com

St. Joseph

IGP Collines Rhodaniennes, Sotanum

Hermitage, Amphore d'Or

18 ha; 450,000 bottles

His interest in the vineyards from Roman times led Pierre Gaillard to start Vins de Vienne together with Yves Cuilleron and François Villard. They began in 1996 by replanting the old vineyards at Seyssuel, just north of Vienne, and then expanded into a negociant business in 1998. They moved to an industrial building close to the Rhône on the outskirts of Chavanay in 2009.

There are more than thirty different wines now, divided into three lines. Archeveque comes from their own vineyards in St. Péray, Cornas, St. Joseph, Condrieu, and Côte Rôtie, as well as the original vineyard in Seyssuel (where Vins de Vienne now owns the ancient château of the archeveque that appears on its label). It's been difficult to acquire vineyards, especially with Condrieu and Côte Rôtie, so some are leased rather than owned.

The negociant wines are divided into two series. Amphora d'Or is the higher level, all with élevage in barriques, typically for 9 months. Amphora d'Argent is the lower level series. The two lines are separate and come from different vineyards (there is no declassification). Vins de Vienne has become a sizeable negociant, but the best wines remain those under the IGP label from the original vineyards at Seyssuel that were the impetus for starting the operation. Those in the Archeveque series offer a good representation of each appellation. The wines of the Amphore d'Or negociant series are distinctly more "serious" than the more approachable wines of the Amphore d'Argent series.

Domaine François Villard

○ 330 route de Réseau Ange, 42410 Saint Michel-sur-Rhône

📞 (33) 04 74 56 83 60

○ François Villard

@ vinsvillard@wanadoo.fr

🌐 www.domainevillard.com

◉ St. Joseph

38 ha; 350,000 bottles

François Villard describes himself as a former chef who was passionate about wine, started by qualifying as a sommelier, and then moved into viticulture and oenology. He planted his first vineyard in 1989 in a small plot in Condrieu. The domain has grown to produce several cuvées from Côte Rôtie, Condrieu, St. Joseph, and St. Péray, as well as several IGPs or Vins de France from declassified lots or from vineyards outside the appellations. The winery was constructed in 1996, then expanded in 2002, and again in 2013.

Altogether François makes red appellation wines from about 14 ha, and white wines from about 11 ha; about 5 ha are in the IGP Collines Rhodaniennes. With around twenty different cuvées, most of the wines are produced only in small amounts, a few thousand bottles at most. The style is rich and modern, although recently it has backed off a bit from new oak. Whites are barrel-fermented; reds are fermented in open-topped wood fermenters or stainless steel. Usually for reds there is only partial destemming.

The style is described as looking for optimal ripening, which in practice means that the whites are often harvested late enough to show a touch of botrytis. In addition to his own domain (relying upon owned and leased vineyards and some purchased grapes), François was one of the gang of three (together with Pierre Gaillard and Yves Cuilleron) who created Vins de Vienne. He's regarded as one of the most enterprising producers in the region.

Domaine Alain Voge   *

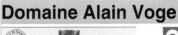

 4 Impasse de l'Equerre, 07130 Cornas

📞 (33) 04 75 40 32 04

 Albéric Mazoyer

@ contact@alain-voge.com

🌐 www.alain-voge.com

◉ Cornas

🍷 Cornas, Vieilles Vignes

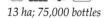

13 ha; 75,000 bottles

Alain Voge is a family estate, run by Alain Voge together with Alberic Mazoyer. "Alain started in the sixties when the small appellations in the Northern Rhône were in very different circumstances from now. The surfaces were decreasing except where the negociants had an interest. Until the seventies, Alain managed a nursery and was a distiller. Things have changed in the last twenty years. It's become possible now to sell Cornas for high prices; this was absolutely impossible before," Alberic says. Alberic has been a friend of the family for more than twenty years, and came from Chapoutier in 2004 to help with the domain.

Behind the modern tasting room at the end of an alley in the center of Cornas is a modern winery (built twelve years ago), small but packed with everything necessary for fine wine production. Everything is aged in barrique, but there is limited use of new oak. Barriques are kept for up to 8 years for the reds, and up to 3 years for the whites. There are 7 ha in Cornas, 4 ha in St. Péray, and 1 ha in St. Joseph, spread among many small parcels.

Alain Voge makes both white and sparkling wines from St. Péray, and reds from Cornas and St. Joseph; for me, the Cornas was the most interesting, especially the Vieilles Vignes, which comes from ten parcels of vines from 30-60 years old, all on granite terraces. Most of the white (95%) is Marsanne, and about 80% is barrel fermented. The style at Alain Voge is pretty taut; in some vintages it can veer towards angularity.

Mini-Profiles of Estates

Domaine Aléofane

745 Avenue du Vercors 26600, Mercurol
(33) 04 75 07 00 82
Natacha Chave
chavenatacha@yahoo.fr

8 ha; 35,000 bottles

Named for a mythical island, the domain was created in 2004 when Natacha Chave left the family estate in Mercurol, run by her brother Yann. There are two wines: St. Joseph comes from a plot of only 1.5 ha; and the main production is Crozes-Hermitages from 40-year-old vines in the plain of Chassis. Wines are aged in a mix of demi-muids and barriques (all used).

Domaine & Maison Alexandrins

Impasse des Pierres - Les Audouards, 26600 Mercurol (Domaine)
23 Place du Taurobole, 26600 Tain l'Hermitage (Maison)
(33) 04 75 08 69 44
Nicolas Perrin
contact@lesalexandrins.com
lesalexandrins.com

10 ha

Les Alexandrins represents the combination of two ventures. Maison Nicolas Perrin was a negociant founded in 2007 and run by Nicolas Jaboulet from premises in Tain l'Hermitage adjacent to the Paul Jaboulet negociant. Domain Les Alexandrins was founded in Mercurol in 2009 by Guillaume Sorrel (son of Marc Sorrel of Domaine Sorrel in Hermitage) and Alexandre Caso. After Les Alexandrins began to provide wine for Maison Nicolas Perrin, the two ventures were formally joined in 2015. Domaine vineyards are in Crozes Hermitage and St. Joseph. The negociant activity extends the range to the other appellation of the northern Rhône as well as to IGP. After initially making wine in other premises, Les Alexandrins now has its own winery in Mercurol.

Domaine Thierry Allemand

22 Impasse des Granges, 07130 Cornas
(33) 04 75 80 07 56
Thierry Allemand
allemand.th@wanadoo.fr

4 ha; 12,000 bottles

Thierry Allemand is one of the producers responsible for the resurrection of Cornas in the 1980s. After working at Domaine Robert Michel, he created his own small domain by clearing and replanting abandoned vineyards. His policy is to harvest late for very ripe fruit. Wines are aged in a mix of foudres and barriques (no new oak), and there are two cuvées: Les Chaillots comes from young vines, and Reynard comes from old vines.

Domaine Gilles Barge

8 Boulevard des Allées, 69420 Ampuis
(33) 04 74 56 13 90
Julien Barge
contact@domainebarge.com
www.domainebarge.com

9 ha

Located right on the main street through Ampuis, this is an old domain (dating from 1860) which has been estate-bottling its wines since 1974. For a small domain (80% in Côte Rôtie), there is a surprisingly wide range of wines. The Côte Rôties are all traditional blends of Syrah with a little Viognier; there's the domain wine, a Côte Brune, a Côte Blonde, and the Le Colombard single vineyard. There is no destemming, and the wines are aged in old demi-muids. There are also two Condrieus, and both red and white from St. Joseph.

Domaine Patrick et Christophe Bonnefond

Mornas, Route de Rozier, 69420 Ampuis
(33) 04 74 56 12 30
Patrick & Christophe Bonnefond
gaec.bonnefond@orange.fr

10 ha; 40,000 bottles

The two brothers took over this family domain at the start of the 1990s. Their parcels on Côte Rôtie are on the Côte Brune, with the wines driven by the terroir of schist. The Rochains and Côte Rozier plots are on either side of La Landonne. The wines are aged in demi-muids and barriques with a little new oak. There is also an IGP, 100% Syrah like the Côte Rôties, which is the bargain of the domain. Viognier comes as Condrieu and as Vin de France.

Domaine Bonserine

2 Chemin de la Viallière, Verenay 69420 Ampuis
(33) 04 74 56 14 27
Ludovic Richard
bonserine@wanadoo.fr
www.domainedebonserine.fr

13 ha; 33,000 bottles

The domain was purchased by Guigal in 2006, but has continued to be run separately. Vineyards are in Côte Rôtie, except for 1 ha in Condrieu. The style is more traditional than Guigal, with wines matured in demi-muids and barriques for long élevage (up to three years). La Sarrasine is the flagship cuvée from Côte Rôtie, and includes 3% Viognier; a blend from eight separate plots, it is up to 90% of production. La Viallière comes from a single parcel and is produced only in top years. La Garde is based on selection of the best lots in top years. In Condrieu there is one cuvée.

Domaine Les Bruyères

12 Chemin du Stade, 26600 Beaumont-Monteux
(33) 04 75 84 74 14
David Reynaud
contact@domainelesbruyeres.fr
www.domainelesbruyeres.fr

23 ha; 140,000 bottles

David Reynaud took his family domain out of the Tain l'Hermitage cooperative in 2003. He has 15 ha in Crozes Hermitage and 6 ha in IGP, and buys grapes from another 8 ha owned by an old friend. Most of the wines come from vineyards on the surrounding Plain de Chassis. In reds, cuvée Georges Reynaud comes from 20-year-old vines and ages in old barriques; Les Croix from 50-year-old vines in a lieu-dit and ages in 4-5-year-old barriques; and Entre Ciel et Terre is made only in top years from old vines, and ages in concrete eggs. There are also two whites from Crozes Hermitage, and a Cornas, and varietal wines under the IGP label.

Domaine Yann Chave

1170 Chemin de La Burge, 26600 Mercurol
(33) 04 75 07 42 11
Yann Chave
chaveyann@yahoo.fr
www.yannchave.com

20 ha; 100,000 bottles

Yann Chave's parents created the domain in 1970 with 4 ha of vines and 3 ha of fruit trees. Grapes went to the cooperative in Tain until estate bottling started in 1978. Yann took over the vineyards in 1996 and stopped producing other crops. Vineyards are all on the plain of Chassis in Crozes Hermitages except for a hectare in Hermitage. The Crozes Hermitage Blanc is 70% Marsanne and 30% Roussanne, and is vinified in cuve to maintain freshness. The red also stays exclusively in cuve. Le Rouvre is a selection of the best lots, often from old vines, and ages in one- and two-year old demi-muids; the Hermitage comes from 40-year-old vines and ages in new and one-year demi muids.

Domaine du Colombier

175 Route des Alpes, 26600 Mercurol
(33) 04 75 07 44 07
Florent & Davide Viale
dom.ducolombier@gmail.com

17 ha; 70,000 bottles

The domain is focused on Crozes-Hermitage and has been bottling its own wine since 1992 (previously the grapes were sold to Guigal). The style of the domain wine is forward and approachable; cuvée Gaby is more "serious," with greater aging potential. There is also an Hermitage from a 2 ha plot on the hill.

Domaine de Corps de Loup

2 Route de Lyon, 69420 Tupin-et-Semons
(33) 09 53 87 84 64
Tristan Daubrée
info@corpsdeloup.com
www.corpsdeloup.com

10 ha

Bruno Daubrée purchased this domain, just at the border between Côte Rôtie and Condrieu, in 1991. Production had been abandoned, and the vineyards had to be restored and replanted. The cellar was renovated in 2007. The vineyards are in Côte Rôtie except for a half hectare in Condrieu and two plots in St. Joseph. The flagship wine is the Corps de Loup Côte Rôtie, 100% Syrah coming from the slopes immediately above the winery. Marions-Les comes from a parcel within the vineyard and is 80% Syrah and 20% Viognier. Paradis comes from farther north, from a parcel in Ampuis on the Côte Brune, and is also 100% Syrah. All cuvées have partial destemming and age for two years in barriques. Tristan Daubrée took over in 2008.

Domaine du Coulet

Le Coulet, 41 et 43 rue du Ruisseau, 07130 Cornas
(33) 04 75 80 08 25
Matthieu Barret
mat-thieu.barret@domaineducoulet.com
domaineducoulet.com

16 ha; 40,000 bottles

Matthieu Barret took his family domain out of the cooperative at Tain l'Hermitage in 2001. He now produces several cuvées from Cornas and a Côtes du Rhone in red, an unusual blend of Viognier and Roussanne that comes from Cornas but as it is white is labeled as Côtes du Rhône, and a red Côtes du Rhône. Cornas Brise Cailloux is a blend from various sites, Les Terrases du Serre comes from 45-year-old vines and is aged in a mix of barriques and concrete eggs, Billes Noires comes from 55-year-old vines and is aged in barriques, and Cornas Gore (Gore is old degraded granite) is a selection from the best parcels of old vines, and is aged in concrete eggs. The red Côtes du Rhône comes from a parcel that Matthieu calls "no man's land," as it lies between the boundaries of Cornas and St. Joseph. Under the negociant label of Matthieu Barret, he extends the range with five more cuvées.

Domaine Courbis

Route de Saint Romain, 07130 Châteaubourg
(33) 04 75 81 81 60
Laurent & Dominique Courbis
contact@domaine-courbis.fr
www.vins-courbis-rhone.com

33 ha; 120,000 bottles

Brothers Laurent and Dominique Courbis produce wines from the southern part of the northern Rhône. The family estate goes back to the sixteenth century. The domain is located at the southern end of St. Joseph, with vineyards on the surrounding slopes, and there are also parcels nearby in Cornas. The white St. Joseph is Marsanne (with 3% Roussanne) and is partly aged in new barriques. The red is aged in barriques with 20% new oak. The Royes cuvées of St. Joseph come from a 6 ha vineyard at the border with Cornas. The Cornas comes from very old vines (planted in 1919). There are also smaller cuvées from St. Péray, Crozes Hermitage, and an IGP from plots adjacent to the Royes vineyard.

Domaine Pierre et Jérôme Coursodon

1 place du Marché, 07300, Mauves
(33) 04 75 08 18 29
Jérôme Coursodon
pierre.coursodon@wanadoo.fr
www.domaine-coursodon.com

15 ha; 60,000 bottles

With vineyards in the heart of the original St. Joseph, mostly in Mauves, the domain regards itself as a reference point for the appellation. The estate was founded by Antonin Coursodon at the end of the nineteenth century, and is now in the fourth and fifth generations with Pierre (viticulturalist) and Jérôme (winemaker). There are two white and four red cuvées, all St. Joseph. Silice is the St. Joseph blend in both white and red. Wines mostly age in old barriques, but Sensonne is a red cuvée that ages in new oak. L'Olivaie is an old vines cuvée and ages in barriques with 15% new. The top cuvée in both red and white is Paradis, which comes from a plot above Mauves.

Domaine Benjamin et David Duclaux

34 Route de Lyon, 69420 Tupin-et-Semons
(33) 04 74 59 56 30
Benjamin Duclaux
contact@coterotie-duclaux.com
www.coterotie-duclaux.com

6 ha; 25,000 bottles

This small family domain was founded in 1928, and is now in the hands of the fourth generation, brothers Benjamin and David. The main cuvée, La Germine, is a classic Côte Blonde blend from several vineyards in the southern part of Côte Rôtie. It includes 3% Viognier and ages in a mix of demi-muids and barriques with 20% new oak. The flagship cuvée is Maison-Rouge, named for the parcel it comes from. This is 100% Syrah and ages in barriques with 40% new oak. La Chana is a new cuvée, introduced in 2014, and intended to be a little lighter, which has 7% Viognier and ages in demi-muids. A Condrieu was also added in 2014 and ages in a mix of cuve and barriques.

Équis

*105 Les Chênes Verts, 26600
Pont-de-l'Isère*
(33) 04 75 55 13 49
Thomas Schmittel
thomas@vinequis.com
www.vinequis.com

5 ha; 50,000 bottles

Équis is the negociant business that Maxime Graillot founded in 2004, in conjunction with his own small domain, called Domaine des Lises. Maxime is the son of Alain Graillot, and since 2008 has made the wines at his father's estate (see profile). The difference in style is that grapes are not destemmed at Alain Graillot, whereas they are destemmed at Équis and Domaine des Lises, so the wines show more overt fruit. The vineyards for Domaine des Lises are at Beaumont-Monteux, just south of the Graillot domain, and make a red Crozes Hermitage. Under the Équis label there are Crozes Hermitage, St. Joseph, and Cornas.

Cave Fayolle Fils & Fille

*9 rue du Ruisseau, 26600
Gervans*
(33) 04 75 03 33 74
Laurent Fayolle & Céline No-din
contact@fayolle-filsetfille.fr
www.fayolle-filsetfille.fr

9 ha; 45,000 bottles

The Fayolle domain was divided into two parts in 2002, and Cave Fayolle today is run by Laurent and Céline, the fifth generation of the Fayolles as winemakers. Located at the northern boundary of Crozes Hermitage, the domain is located in the center of the village of Gervans. (The other part of the original Fayolle domain has a tasting room on RN7.) Cuvées from Crozes Hermitage, both red and white, are divided into Sens (a blend from several terroirs) and Le Pentaire (the flagship wine specifically from more stony terroir). The top red is Le Cornirets, which comes from a 1 ha parcel of 60-year-old vines on granite in the village of Crozes, aged in barriques with a third new oak. There is also a small production of Hermitage.

Domaine André François

*340 Chemin de Mornas, 69420
Ampuis: (33) 04 74 56 13 80
André François
francois.ded@wanadoo.fr
www.coterotie-andrefrancois.com*

 3 ha

André François founded the domain at the end of the 1980s with only 0.25 ha. The estate remains very small, but has a classic range of wines: Côte Rôtie (the Cuvée Classique is blend from several plots, while Gérine comes from a single parcel at the northern boundary), Condrieu, and an IGP from outside the appellation. All wines are aged for two years in barriques.

Domaine Garon

*58 Route de la Taquière, 69420
Ampuis*
*(33) 04 74 56 14 11
Jean-Francois Garon
vins@domainegaron.fr
www.domainegaron.fr*

8 ha; 38,000 bottles

The first Garon to make wine was in the fifteenth century, but the domain was founded more recently, by Jean-François and Carmen in 1982, when they replanted family vineyards that had been abandoned. Today they produce four cuvées, each representing different terroirs of Côte Rôtie. Les Triotes was the first cuvée, in 1995 (originally labeled just Domaine Garon Côte Rôtie), and is a blend from three plots of schist in Côte Blonde. Lancement is a single parcel on schist. La Sybarine comes from granite plots in the southern end of Côte Rôtie. Les Rochins comes from a single parcel of schist in the Côte Brune. Each cuvée is exclusively Syrah; there is partial destemming, and wines are aged in barriques with new oak depending on the cuvée.

Domaine Pierre Gonon

34 Avenue Ozier, 07300 Mauves
(33) 04 75 08 45 27
Pierre Gonon
gonon.pierre@wanadoo.fr

9 ha; 40,000 bottles

Pierre Gonon established the reputation of this domain with his vineyards on the slopes of Mauves in the heart of the old St. Joseph appellation. Since 1989 it has been run by his sons, Jean and Pierre. All the vineyards are on granitic terroir, including the most recent purchase, in 2005, of a vineyard from Raymond Trollat when he retired. The white (Les Oliviers) is 80% Marsanne and 20% Roussanne and comes from a block facing Hermitage (on the other side of the river). It ages in demi-muid and barriques. The red comes from Tournon, Mauves and St Jean de Muzols ; it is partially destemmed and aged in a mix of foudres and demi-muids. There are also an IGP red (Les Iles Feray) and a Vin de France from a tiny plot of Chasselas.

Domaine Bernard Gripa

5 Avenue Ozier, 07300 Mauves
(33) 04 75 08 14 96
Fabrice Gripa
gripa@wanadoo.fr

16 ha; 80,000 bottles

One of the well-known domains in Mauves, in the heart of the St. Joseph appellation, Bernard Gripa made the transition from grower to wine producer in 1974. Bernard's son Fabrice took over in 1993. Vineyards are half red and half white, in St. Joseph except for 3.5 ha of the white in St. Péray. In St. Péray, Les Pins is 80% Marsanne and vinified in cuve, while Les Figuiers is 70% Roussanne and vinified in barriques with 15% new oak. In St. Joseph there are two cuvées each of red and white; in each the top cuvée is called Le Berceau (which literally means "the cradle," referring to the position of the vineyards in Mauves). The white is 100% Marsanne. The red comes from a hectare of the oldest vines.

Domaine Philippe et Vincent Jaboulet

920 Route de la Négociale, 26600
Mercurol
(33) 04 75 07 44 32
Philippe & Vincent Jaboulet
jabouletphilippeetvincent@wanadoo.fr
www.jaboulet-philippe-vincent.fr

30 ha; 110,000 bottles

After the family firm of Jaboulet was sold in 2006 (see profile), Philippe together with his son Vincent established his own domain, with small holdings in Hermitage (less than a hectare each of red and white), the major part of the domain in Crozes Hermitage (including 11 ha of the Thalabert vineyard from the old Jaboulet family estate), and a small vineyard in Cornas. The Crozes Hermitage is aged mostly in vat, with 20% in wood of various sizes, but no new oak. The Nouvelère cuvée comes from 80-year-old vines in Thalabert, and is aged in a mixture of foudres and barriques, including some new oak. The Ermitage red (the Jaboulets use the old spelling, without the "H") comes from 40-year-old vines and ages in barriques, half new; the white is 100% Roussanne. The Cornas is treated like the Ermitage red.

Vignobles Levet

26 Boulevard-des-Allées, 69420 Ampuis
(33) 04 74 56 15 39
Agnès Levet
contact@coterotielevet.fr
www.coterotielevet.fr

5 ha; 20,000 bottles

Founded in 1929, this small domain located in the center of Ampuis took its modern form under Bernard Levet in 1983, and has been run by his daughter Agnès since 2014. Vineyards are in half a dozen plots on Côte Rôtie, with vines mostly more than 40-years-old that are perpetuated by selection massale. There are three cuvées. Améthyste is the classic assemblage from the vineyards, Maestria comes from La Landonne, and La Péroline from lieu-dit Chavaroche . Winemaking is traditional: there is no destemming, aging starts in large vats, and is continued in demi-muids.

Domaine Jean-Claude Marsanne

18 Chemin de Halage, 07300 Mauves
(33) 09 81 01 46 87
Jean-Claude Marsanne
cavemarsanne@aol.com
www.domainemarsanne.com

7 ha; 30,000 bottles

This old domain focuses on red wine from Mauves and Tournon, so the principal cuvée is a St. Joseph, aged in demi-muids and barriques with 15% new oak. However, there is also a red cuvée from Crozes Hermitage, a white cuvée from St. Joseph, and an IGP Ardèche from Viognier. The wine is well represented in local restaurants.

Domaine Michelas Saint-Jemms

557 Route de Bellevue, 26600 Mercurol
(33) 04 75 07 86 70
Sylvie Chevrol-Michelas
michelas.st.jemms@wanadoo.fr
www.michelas-st-jemms.fr

51 ha; 120,000 bottles

Quite a sizeable domain for the region, Michelas has vineyards in Hermitage, Crozes Hermitage, St. Joseph, and Cornas. There is perhaps a certain lack of focus, with wines divided into three ranges: sweet wines from IGP Collines Rhodaniennes together with fruit juices; red and white wines from Crozes Hermitage, St. Joseph, and Cornas , labeled as Les Valeurs Sûres; and the top wines, under the Terres d'Arce name, all red, one from each appellation. Wines are aged in old barriques. The tasting room is always open.

Domaine du Murinais

1890 Route du Laboureur, 26600 Beaumont-Monteux
04 75 07 34 76
Luc Tardy
contact@domainedumurinais.com
www.domainedumurinais.com

17 ha; 65,000 bottles

Grapes were sent to the cooperative for many years, until Luc Tardy created the domain by renovating the cave and starting estate bottling in 1998. Vineyards are all local in the southern part of Crozes Hermitage, and there are three red cuvées and one white. Les Amandiers comes from younger vines (less than 20-years-old) and is aged in a mixture of concrete and old demi-muids, Vieilles Vignes comes from 30-45-year-old vines and is aged in demi-muids of 2-4-years age, and Caprice de Valentin comes from 45-year-old vines and is aged in new demi-muids. The white is an equal blend of Marsanne and Roussanne and is aged in concrete eggs.

Domaine Vincent Paris

*Chemin des Peyrouses, 07130
Cornas*
(33) 04 75 40 13 04
Vincent Paris
vinparis@wanadoo.fr
vin-paris.fr

8 ha; 40,000 bottles

Vincent Paris started making wine with his uncle, Robert Michel, and then established his own domain in 1997 with vineyards inherited from his grandfather (where the vines are very old) and rented from his uncle (who retired in 2006). The winery is a modern, warehouse-like, building. Cornas is the heart of the domain, with Granit 30 coming from young vines that Vincent planted ten years ago, Granit 60 coming from vines of 30-100-years-old, and La Geynale representing a single parcel. There's also a red from St. Joseph and a Viognier IGP. Under the Vincent Paris Selections label, there's also Crozes Hermitage from vineyards Vincent manages but does not own.

Domaine du Pavillon

*250, Chemin des Ecoles,, 26600
Mercurol*
(33) 04 75 07 99 12
Stéphane Cornu
le-domaine-du-pavillon@wanadoo.fr
www.pavillon-mercurol.fr

13 ha; 20,000 bottles

When Vital Cornu purchased the estate in 1961, it was a farm of fruit trees. It was slowly converted to vineyards, and when Stéphane took over in 1990, he completed the conversion and started estate-bottling. Both the red and white Crozes Hermitage—there is one cuvée of each—are aged in barriques. Under the label N7 (the number of the main road near the domain), the wines are also available in 10 liter bag-in-box.

Domaine Pichat

*6 Chemin de La Viallière, 69420
Ampuis*
(33) 04 74 48 37 23
Stéphane Pichat
info@domainepichat.com
www.domainepichat.com

5 ha; 20,000 bottles

This tiny domain was only 2 ha before Stéphane Pichat started to bottle his wine in 2000, beginning with only 900 bottles. Vineyards are divided into several locations on Côte Rôtie, and the three cuvées express different terroirs: Löss comes from loess, Champons from schist, and Grandes Places comes from a single parcel in the lieu dit. A Vin de France Syrah is declassified from two parcels. In whites, there's Condrieu and a Vin de France Viognier from parcels on Côte Rôtie. The style is modernist, with all wines aged in 400 liter barriques of 1-2-years age, with 30-40% new oak for Champons, and 100% new oak for Grandes Places.

Domaine Christophe Pichon

36 le Grand-Val, Lieu-dit Verlieu, 42410 Chavanay
(33) 04 74 87 06 78
Christophe Pichon
chrpichon@wanadoo.fr
www.domaine-pichon.fr

20 ha; 100,000 bottles

Christophe took over the domain in 1991 and began to expand it. A new cave was constructed in 2010. His son Corentin joined the domain in 2014. Vineyards are divided roughly equally between Condrieu, Côte Rôtie, and St. Joseph, with smaller holdings in Cornas and IGP. The style is modern and relatively extracted; the three Côte Rôtie cuvées are mostly aged in new oak, St. Joseph in barriques of up to 4-years age, Condrieu in a mix of new and 1-year oak, and Cornas in new and 1-2-year barriques.

Julien Pilon

8 rue Cuvillière, 69420, Condrieu
(33) 06 75 77 55 66
Julien Pilon
info@julienpilon.fr
www.julienpilon.fr

13 ha; 60,000 bottles

Julien started with the 2010 vintage, made on a small scale in his parents' garage, spent a period at Pierre-Jean Villa, and then established his own domain in Condrieu, specializing in dry white wines. Estate wines come from parcels on Côte Rôtie and Condrieu, but most of the cuvées come from purchased grapes. There are whites from Condrieu, Hermitage, Crozes Hermitage, and St. Joseph, all aged in old barriques, with an emphasis on freshness.

Domaine Pochon

80 Chemin des Pierres, 26600
Chanos-Curson
(33) 04 75 07 34 60
Etienne Pochon
domainespochon@wanadoo.fr
www.chateaucurson.fr

16 ha; 80,000 bottles

Étienne Pochon took his family estate out of the cooperative and started estate bottling in 1988. The red and white Crozes Hermitage are labeled as Domaine Pochon. The white is a more or less equal blend of Marsanne and Roussanne. Château Curson is the name of the Pochon family estate (the château itself has medieval cellars) and is used for the top wine, which comes from older vines around the château.

Domaine Gilles Robin

55 Chemin des Sarments. Les Châs-
sis-Sud, 26600 Mercurol
(33) 04 75 08 43 28
Gilles Robin
gillesrobin@wanadoo.fr
www.gillesrobin.com

15 ha; 80,000 bottles

The estate was planted in the 1940s by Gilles Robin's grandparents, and grapes were sold to the cooperative until Gilles started bottling in 1995. Vineyards are just to the south of Hermitage. The white Crozes Hermitage is 40% Marsanne and 60% Roussanne and ages half in vat and half in old barriques. Intended for early drinking, the red Cuvée du Papillon comes from younger vines, which Gilles planted in 1996, and ages in vat. Cuvée Albert Bouvet is named for Gilles' grandfather and comes from 40-year-old vines near the hill of Hermitage. There is now also an Hermitage.

Domaine de la Côte Sainte Epine

17 Chemin de La Cote Sainte Epine,
07300 Saint Jean de Muzols
(33) 04 75 08 85 35
Mickaël Desestret
mikael.desestret@yahoo.fr

7 ha; 25,000 bottles

Located in the heart of the St. Joseph appellation, the domain is known for its very old vines (the oldest are 140-years- old), including some plots that come from the old Raymond Trollat estate. "The old vines have a tiny production, but I keep them because of the quality," Mickaël Desestret says. Together with his father, he produces only two cuvées: one red St. Joseph (almost 90% of total production) and one white (100% Marsanne). Winemaking is traditional, with no new oak, but the style is rich and concentrated.

Domaine Jean-Michel Stéphan

1 Ancienne Route de Semons-Tupin (RN86), 69420 Tupin-Semons
(33) 04 74 56 62 66
Jean-Michel &Stéphan
jean-michel.stephan3@wanadoo.fr

6 ha; 14,000 bottles

Jean-Michel has acquired a reputation as purist. Founding his own domain with three plots in Côte Rôtie in 1991, he focused on Sérine (the old variety of Syrah) in the vineyards, winemaking with no new oak, and minimal, or even zero, use of sulfur. The cuvée En Coteaux Vieilles Vignes comes exclusively from Sérine. Reflecting time spent in Beaujolais, his generic Côte Rôtie is made more approachable by using some carbonic maceration: for this reason it was judged atypical and denied the *agrément* for the AOP one year: it was bottled as a Vin de France under the name VSO (vin sans origine). There are also Condrieu and an IGP Viognier from a plot on the plain near Condrieu. The latest news, Jean-Michel says, is that his oldest son has now joined the domain, and in 2018 they are planting another 5 ha of several varieties in different terroirs and communes.

Cave de Tain

22 Route de Larnage, 26600 Tain l'Hermitage
(33) 04 75 08 20 87
Xavier Gomart
contact@cavedetain.com
www.cavedetain.com

985 ha; 5,000,000 bottles

Founded in 1933, this is the most important cooperative in the Northern Rhône, making wine from more than a quarter of the vineyards. All the appellations are included and there are also varietal wines from the IGP Collines Rhodaniennes. In addition to the appellation wines per se, there are several single-vineyard cuvées, and some organic wines. Most of the grapes come from members of the cooperative, of course, but the Cave owns some vineyards, including 21 ha of Hermitage (which came from the estate of Louis Gambert de Loche who founded the cooperative). The Cave is a huge modern building in Tain l'Hermitage, just beside the hill of Hermitage, with a boutique and tasting room.

Pierre-Jean Villa

5, Route de Pélussin, 42410 Chavanay
(33) 04 74 54 41 10
Pierre-Jean Villa
contact@pierre-jean-villa.com
www.pierre-jean-villa.com

13 ha; 50,000 bottles

Pierre-Jean made wine in Burgundy, returned to his native Rhône in 2003 to manage the Vins de Vienne, and then founded his own domain in 2009. The Côte Rôtie Carmina comes from 20-year-old vines; Bell de Maïa comes from 60-year-old vines but is made only in top years. There are both red and white from St. Joseph (Tildé is a red cuvée from old vines; the white Saut de l'Ange is 100% Roussanne), a Condrieu, and red Crozes Hermitage. Destemming depends on vintage, and wines are aged in a mixture of barriques and demi-muids. Together with Olivier Decelle (of Mas Amiel in the Languedoc) Pierre-Jean also created Decelle-Villa, a 7 ha estate in Burgundy.

Index of Estates by Rating

4 star

Domaine Jean-Louis Chave

3 star

Domaine Clape

Maison Guigal

Domaine René Rostaing

Domaine Marc Sorrel

2 star

Domaine Belle

Maison Clusel Roch

Domaine Jean-Luc Colombo

Domaine Combier

Cave Yves Cuilleron

Maison Delas Frères

Maison Michel Ferraton Père & Fils

Domaine Pierre Gaillard

Domaine Jean-Michel Gerin

Domaine Alain Graillot

Château Grillet

Domaines Paul Jaboulet Aîné

Domaine Jamet

Domaine Jasmin

Domaine Michel et Stéphane Ogier

Domaine Georges Vernay

1 star

Domaine Franck Balthazar

Maison Chapoutier Vins Fins

Domaine André Perret

Domaine des Remizières

Domaine Eric Texier

Domaine du Tunnel

Maison Vidal-Fleury

Les Vins de Vienne

Domaine François Villard

Domaine Alain Voge

Index of Organic and Biodynamic Estates

Domaine Aléofane

Domaine Thierry Allemand

Domaine Franck Balthazar

Domaine Belle

Domaine Les Bruyères

Maison Chapoutier Vins Fins

Domaine Yann Chave

Maison Clusel Roch

Domaine Combier

Domaine du Coulet

Équis

Maison Michel Ferraton Père & Fils

Domaine Pierre Gonon

Domaine Alain Graillot

Domaines Paul Jaboulet Aîné

Domaine Pochon

Domaine Jean-Michel Stéphan

Domaine Eric Texier

Domaine Georges Vernay

Domaine Alain Voge

Index of Estates by Appellation

Crozes-Hermitage
Domaine Aléofane
Domaine Belle
Domaine Les Bruyères
Domaine Yann Chave
Domaine du Colombier
Domaine Combier
Équis
Cave Fayolle Fils & Fille
Domaine Philippe et Vincent Jaboulet
Domaine Michelas Saint-Jemms
Domaine du Murinais
Domaine du Pavillon
Domaine Pochon
Domaine des Remizières
Domaine Gilles Robin

Hermitage
Domaine & Maison Alexandrins
Maison Chapoutier Vins Fins
Maison Michel Ferraton Père & Fils
Domaines Paul Jaboulet Aîné
Domaine Marc Sorrel
Cave de Tain

St. Joseph
Domaine Jean-Louis Chave
Domaine Pierre et Jérôme Coursodon
Maison Delas Frères
Domaine Pierre Gaillard
Domaine Pierre Gonon
Domaine Alain Graillot
Domaine Bernard Gripa
Domaine Jean-Claude Marsanne
Domaine de la Côte Sainte Epine
Les Vins de Vienne
Pierre-Jean Villa
Domaine François Villard

St. Péray
Domaine du Tunnel

Index of Estates by Name

Books by Benjamin Lewin MW

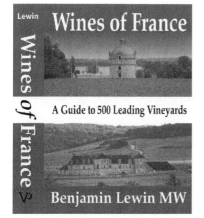

Wines of France

This comprehensive account of the vineyards and wines of France today is extensively illustrated with photographs and maps of each wine-producing area. Leading vineyards and winemakers are profiled in detail, with suggestions for wines to try and vineyards to visit.

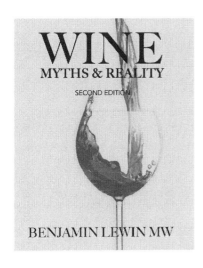

Wine Myths and Reality

Extensively illustrated with photographs, maps, and charts, this behind-the-scenes view of winemaking reveals the truth about what goes into a bottle of wine. Its approachable and entertaining style immediately engages the reader in the wine universe.

Made in the USA
Columbia, SC
20 January 2018